Microsoft® Office
PowerPoint® 2007

VISUAL™
Quick Tips

Visual®

by Paul McFedries

BICENTENNIAL
1807
WILEY
2007
BICENTENNIAL

Wiley Publishing, Inc.

Microsoft® Office PowerPoint® 2007 VISUAL™ Quick Tips

Published by
Wiley Publishing, Inc.
111 River Street
Hoboken, NJ 07030-5774

Published simultaneously in Canada

Copyright © 2007 by Wiley Publishing, Inc.,
Indianapolis, Indiana

Library of Congress Control Number: 2006936750

ISBN-13: 978-0-470-08973-6

ISBN-10: 0-470-08973-3

Manufactured in the United States of America

10 9 8 7 6 5 4 3 2 1

1K/RT/RS/QW/IN

Trademark Acknowledgments

Contact Us

For general information on our other products and services contact our Customer Care Department within the U.S. at 800-762-2974, outside the U.S. at 317-572-3993, or fax 317-572-4002.

For technical support, please visit www.wiley.com/techsupport.

WILEY

Wiley Publishing, Inc.

Sales

Contact Wiley at (800) 762-2974 or fax (317) 572-4002.

Praise for Visual Books

Credits

Project Editor
Jade L. Williams

Acquisitions Editor
Jody Lefevere

Product Development Supervisor
Courtney Allen

Technical Editor
Lee Musick

Editorial Manager
Robyn Siesky

Business Manager
Amy Knies

Editorial Assistant
Laura Sinise

Manufacturing
Allan Conley
Linda Cook
Paul Gilchrist
Jennifer Guynn

Book Design
Kathie S. Rickard

Production Coordinator
Adrienne Martinez

Layout
LeAndra Hosier
Melanee Prendergast

Screen Artist
Jill A. Proll

Illustrators
Ronda David-Burroughs
Cheryl Grubbs

Cover Design
Anthony Bunyan

Proofreaders
Jessica Kramer
Henry Lazarek

Indexer
Kevin Broccoli

Special Help
Tim Borek
Jenny Watson

Vice President and Executive Group Publisher
Richard Swadley

Vice President Publisher
Barry Pruett

Composition Director
Debbie Stailey

About the Author

Paul McFedries is the president of Logophilia Limited, a technical writing company. While now primarily a writer, Paul has worked as a programmer, consultant, and Web site developer. Paul has written nearly 50 books that have sold more than three million copies worldwide. These books include the Wiley titles *Windows XP: Top 100 Simplified Tips and Tricks*, 2nd Edition, and *Teach Yourself VISUALLY Computers*, 4th Edition. Paul also runs Word Spy, a Web site dedicated to tracking new words and phrases (see www.wordspy.com).

How To Use This Book

Microsoft Office PowerPoint® 2007 VISUAL Quick Tips includes 124 tasks that reveal cool secrets, teach timesaving tricks, and explain great tips guaranteed to make you more productive with PowerPoint. The easy-to-use layout lets you work through all the tasks from beginning to end or jump in at random.

Who Is This Book For?

You already know PowerPoint basics. Now you'd like to go beyond, with shortcuts, tricks, and tips that let you work smarter and faster. And because you learn more easily when someone *shows* you how, this is the book for you.

Conventions Used In This Book

❶ Introduction
The introduction is designed to get you up to speed on the topic at hand.

❷ Steps
This book uses step-by-step instructions to guide you easily through each task. Numbered callouts on every screen shot show you exactly how to perform each task, step by step.

❸ Tips
Practical tips provide insights to save you time and trouble, caution you about hazards to avoid, and reveal how to do things with PowerPoint that you never thought possible!

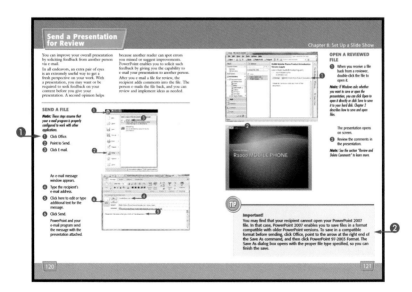

In order to get this information to you in a timely manner, this book was based on a pre-release version of Microsoft Vista/Microsoft Office 2007. There may be some minor changes between the screenshots in this book and what you see on your desktop. As always, Microsoft has the final word on how programs look and function; if you have any questions or see any discrepancies, consult the online help for further information about the software.

Table of Contents

chapter 1 — Working with Outlines

chapter 2 — Working with Slide Content

chapter 3 — Using Themes

chapter **4** **Using Masters**

chapter **5** **Adding Graphics and Drawings**

chapter **6** Organizing Slides

chapter **7** Adding Action to Slides

chapter **8**
Set Up a Slide Show

chapter **9**
Print Presentations

chapter **10** **Publish Presentations**

chapter **11** **Finalizing and Making a Presentation**

chapter **12** **Making a Photo Album**

chapter 13 Customizing PowerPoint

Working with Outlines

The Outline tab provides the easiest and most convenient place to enter presentation text. The Outline tab helps you organize your thoughts into a simple outline hierarchy so that you can focus on idea flow in your presentation. You can make changes to text here quickly, too.

You can enter presentation text in the Outline tab, or directly on a slide in the Slide pane in Normal view. You can work more effectively when you understand how the contents of the outline and each slide placeholder relate.

Every top-level heading – that is, a heading at level 1 in the outline – is the title of a slide. When you type text in a title placeholder on a slide, it appears as a level 1 heading in the outline. When you type a level 1 heading in the outline, it appears in the title placeholder on the slide.

The second level of headings in an outline becomes the bullets in the content placeholder on the corresponding slide. If you have more than one level of bullets in the outline, there will be multiple levels of bullets on the slide, and vice versa.

As you see in this chapter, using PowerPoint's Outline pane, you can build your presentation from scratch by entering outline text directly. You can promote or demote items to different levels using shortcut keys.

Quick Tips

Enter Presentation Content in an Outline

You can build the text for a new presentation in moments on the Outline tab. In PowerPoint, outlines offer a convenient way of organizing the content of your presentation hierarchically: The top level of the outline hierarchy consists of the slide titles; the second level of the outline hierarchy consists of the subtitle in the first slide and the main bullet points in

subsequent slides; and lower levels of the outline hierarchy consist of the lower levels of bullet points in subsequent slides.

By typing your slide text and using keystrokes such as Enter, Tab, and Shift+Tab, you can define the text for an entire presentation right from your keyboard.

---

1 Create a new, blank presentation file.

The blank presentation appears in Normal view.

2 Click the Outline tab.

3 Click in the outline beside the first slide icon.

4 Type a line of text.

5 Press Enter.

● A second blank slide and slide icon appear.

6 Type a second line of text.

The text becomes the title of the second slide.

7 Press Enter.

8 Press Tab.

● The insertion point moves right becoming the first bullet in the text placeholder on the second slide.

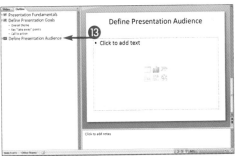

⑨ Type text for the first bullet item.

⑩ Press Enter.

⑪ Repeat steps **9** and **10** to add bullet items as needed.

⑫ When you want to start a new slide, press Shift+Tab.

● The insertion point moves left, which is also considered up, one level to become the title for the new slide.

⑬ Type the title for the new slide.

⑭ Continue adding slides and bulleted lists, using Tab and Shift+Tab to create bulleted lists and new slides as needed.

More Options!

If you have long text entries, you can enlarge the outline pane. Move the mouse pointer over the splitter bar at the right edge of the pane and drag the bar to the right. Notice that the Slide pane shrinks in size to accommodate the change. To reduce the size of the left pane again, drag to the left. If you drag too far, the pane disappears, but you can click the View tab, and then click Normal on the Ribbon.

You can use the Outline tab to easily rearrange your slides and create a more effective presentation.

As with other types of document content, presentation content evolves in drafts. When you enter the text for your presentation in the Outline tab, the order you add the slides may not be ideal after the first draft. For example, you may review your presentation and decide on a more logical or coherent flow for the information. Fortunately, the order you enter the slides is not fixed, which means you can rearrange your slides as needed at any time. PowerPoint enables you to reorder the slides in your outline by dragging and dropping them within the Outline tab.

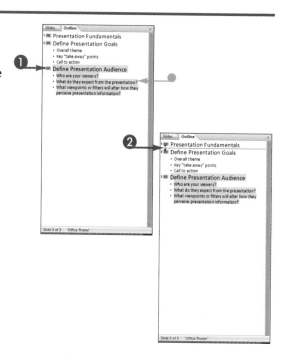

① Click the Slide icon for the slide you want to move in the Outline tab.

● The icon and all the slide text are highlighted in the Outline tab.

② Drag the icon until the horizontal line representing its outline position reaches the desired position.

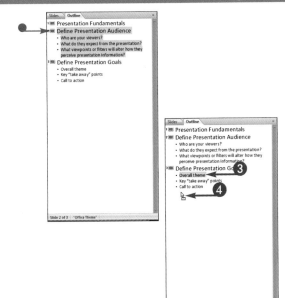

● When you release the mouse button, the entire slide moves up or down in the outline.

③ Click the bullet for a bullet item or triple-click the bullet text to select it.

Either method selects the entire bullet item.

④ Drag the bullet item to a new location in the bulleted list.

When you release the mouse button, the bullet item moves up or down and can even move from one slide to another.

TIP

More Options!

You can also move lines of text up or down in an outline using the keyboard. Click the heading and press Alt+Shift+Up arrow to move it up in the outline, or press Alt+Shift+Down arrow to move the heading down in the outline. There are also button commands for moving a selection in the Outline tab. You can add Move Up and Move Down buttons to the Quick Access toolbar. See the section "Customize the Quick Access Toolbar" in Chapter 13 to learn how to do so.

Promote and Demote Items

You can use the Outline tab to easily promote and demote items to get the optimum structure for your slides.

The Outline tab's big picture view not only lets you easily see the overall organization of your presentation, it also makes modifying that organization easy. That is, by editing the outline, you also edit the organization. Besides editing the text itself, you can also change the outline levels. Changing levels means moving items down or up within the outline hierarchy. To *demote* an item means to move it lower in the hierarchy (for example, from second level to third); to *promote* an item means to move it higher in the hierarchy (for example, from second level to top level). You can promote and demote text by using the Ribbon or the mouse.

---

① Click the Home tab.

② Click the Outline tab, if needed.

③ Click anywhere in a heading.

④ Click the Decrease List Level button.

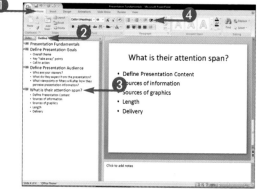

● The heading moves down one level in the outline hierarchy.

⑤ Click anywhere in a bulleted item other than a level 1 heading.

⑥ Click the Increase List Level button.

You can click Decrease List Level and Increase List Level more than once to move the heading more than one level in the outline.

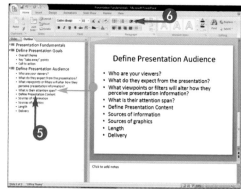

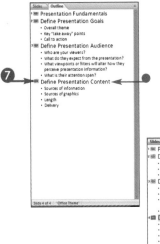

● The heading moves up one level in the outline hierarchy.

⑦ Click the Slide icon or the bullet for a bulleted list item to select the slide or that bullet item.

⑧ Right-click the selection.

⑨ Click Promote or Demote.

PowerPoint promotes or demotes the text in the outline.

If you click the Slide icon to select the whole slide, PowerPoint demotes each line in the slide by one level.

More Options!

You can also use keyboard shortcuts for promoting or demoting headings in a PowerPoint outline. Click in a heading or bullet item in the Outline pane. Press Tab to demote the text, or press Shift+Tab to promote it.

Collapse and Expand an Outline

You can control the amount of detail shown in the Outline tab by collapsing and expanding the outline as needed.

If you are working with a long presentation, the Outline pane might show only a small number of the slides. To keep the big picture in view, you can tell PowerPoint to show less outline detail. For example, you can collapse an outline so that you see only slide titles.

Similarly, collapsing subheadings helps you to scroll through the presentation more quickly in the Outline tab. PowerPoint also enables you to quickly expand parts of an outline to look at the details on one or more slides.

You also can collapse or expand a specific set of slides by selecting them before using these steps.

---

① In the Outline tab, right-click a slide title or bullet item with subheads beneath it.

② Click Collapse.

PowerPoint collapses all text but the slide title and displays a gray underline under the title with collapsed text.

If an additional submenu appears, you can ignore it when expanding and collapsing.

③ Right-click a collapsed title or heading.

④ Click Expand.

The slide text reappears.

Double-click the Slide icon for any slide to collapse or expand it.

● If you point to Collapse or Expand on the shortcut menu, you then can click Collapse All or Expand All to hide or redisplay all slide text (displaying slide titles only as needed).

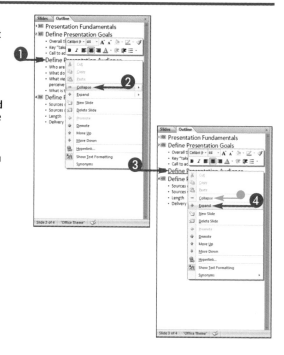

You can use the Outline tab to quickly edit the text for your slide titles, subtitles, or bullets.

Professionals never settle for the first draft. You will typically want to edit presentation text to polish it, to make your prose more forceful or persuasive,

or to make long-winded bullets more succinct. You will also want to edit the presentation text to fix typos, factual errors, grammatical mistakes, or other problems. Editing an outline is much like editing text anyplace else in PowerPoint or in any other application.

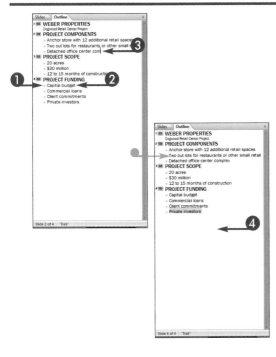

① Click at the point where you want to add or delete text.

② Add or delete the text.

Pressing Delete deletes the letter to the right of your insertion point.

Pressing Backspace deletes the text to the left of your insertion point.

③ Select text anywhere in a slide title or bullet item and type replacement text.

④ Click the bullet for any bullet item to select the entire bullet.

● Optionally, you can click the Slide icon to select an entire slide.

⑤ Press Delete.

The entire slide or the full bullet item is deleted.

Insert Slides from an Outline

Though you can create an outline in moments using PowerPoint's Outline tab, you need not reinvent the wheel if you have already written an outline in Microsoft Word or in another PowerPoint presentation. You can import an outline from another file to supply all or part of the content for a new presentation, and then edit and format it as usual.

In particular, you can convert Word's own outline hierarchy — the styles Heading 1, Heading 2, and so on — into a PowerPoint outline. PowerPoint interprets a Heading 1 style as a top-level item in a presentation outline. Similarly, PowerPoint interprets a Heading 2 style as a second-level item in a presentation outline. So each paragraph of Heading 2 text becomes a main bullet (or subtitle) in the presentation.

---

① Click Office.

② Click Open.

③ Click All PowerPoint Presentations.

④ Click All Outlines.

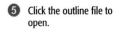

5 Click the outline file to open.

6 Click Open.

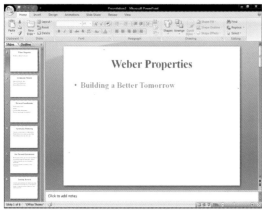

The new presentation appears in the Normal view.

Watch Out!

If you want to build a presentation from a Word outline, PowerPoint will not convert the Word document if that document is open elsewhere. Therefore, be sure to close the Word document before attempting to import the outline. Remember, too, that each top-level heading in the imported outline becomes the title for a new slide. So be sure to review the outline before importing it and promote each heading that you see as a slide title to the top level in the outline.

Working with Slide Content

Most presentation slides combine a slide title, slide text in the form of a bulleted list or table, and graphic elements. The slide layout that you select determines where the title, text, and graphics will appear. You can create a presentation quickly using the available slide layouts.

The layout gallery enables you to choose the slide layout to use for a slide. The gallery offers layouts that hold text only. These include the Title Slide, Section Header, and Title Only layouts. Other layouts include a title plus content placeholders for bulleted lists or graphic contents. You can insert any one of six types of graphic elements, such as a chart

or picture, or a bulleted list into a content placeholder. The Title and Content, Two Content, Comparison, and Content with Caption have content placeholders. Two additional slide layouts – Blank and Picture with Caption – appear in the gallery.

Each slide layout offers a prearranged set of placeholders. Each placeholder can contain either text or a graphic element, but not both. You can click in a text placeholder and type or edit text. You can click in a content placeholder and use the icons in it to insert a visual element. You can also move placeholders around the slide to design a more attractive arrangement.

Quick Tips

If you want a new slide with a particular layout, you can save a step by choosing the desired layout when you insert the slide.

The easiest way to add a new slide to your presentation is to click the top portion of the New Slide button. When you do this for the first time in a new presentation, PowerPoint inserts a slide with the Title and Content layout. If this is not the

layout you want, then you need to change the layout, as described in the next task. To avoid having to change the layout, you can insert the new slide using the layout you prefer.

Note that after you insert a slide with a different layout, clicking the top portion of the New Slide button inserts a new slide using that recent layout.

① Select the slide after which you want to insert the new slide.

Note: *Remember that the method you use to select the slide will vary depending on the current view.*

② Click the Home tab.

③ Click the bottom portion of the New Slide button.

The layout gallery appears.

④ Click the desired layout.

● The new slide with the specified layout appears in the presentation.

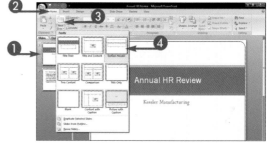

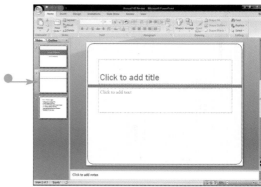

Change a Slide Layout

You can ensure that your slides display the content you want by changing the slide layout to one that includes the placeholders your content requires.

PowerPoint offers several different slide layouts, and not every layout may be appropriate for the content you want to display on a slide. If you decide a slide's original layout no longer works, you can

apply a different slide layout in Normal view or Slide Sorter view.

If you select a layout that does not include an element from the original layout — such as a chart that you have set up — PowerPoint will keep that additional element on the slide, even with the new layout.

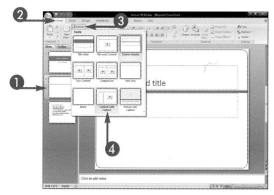

① Select the slide for which you to change the layout.

② Click the Home tab.

③ Click the Layout button.

The layout gallery appears.

④ Click the new slide layout to apply.

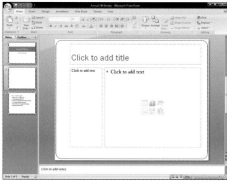

The slide you selected in step 1 changes to use the new layout.

You can make certain kinds of data more readable and easier to understand by displaying that data within a table embedded in a slide.

A *table* is a rectangular arrangement of rows and columns, where each column contains a particular type of data (such as a name or address) and each row is a particular instance of the data (such as a person). A table enables you to arrange information in rows and columns for easy data comparison. For example, you may list regions of the country in the far left column, with the remaining columns presenting sales by year for each region. You can use a content placeholder to insert a table, and then type labels and data into the table cells.

INSERT A TABLE

① On a slide with a content placeholder, click the Insert Table icon.

The Insert Table dialog box appears.

② Click here to set the number of columns.

③ Click here to set the number of rows.

④ Click OK.

The table appears on the slide, with a table style pre-applied.

By default, most of the table styles assume you will enter column headings (labels) in the top row of the table.

TYPE TEXT IN A TABLE

⑤ Type a column heading in the first cell.

⑥ Press Tab.

The insertion point moves to the next cell.

⑦ Continue making cell entries, pressing Tab after each.

⑧ Click outside the table.

The finished table appears on your slide.

● To make a change in table data, you can click the cell to edit, placing the insertion point in the cell. Use the keyboard to make desired changes, and then click outside the table to finish.

Change It!

You can add rows (or columns) to a table. You can use the commands on the shortcut menu that appear when you right-click a table to insert rows. Right-click a table row or column, and then point to Insert. In the shortcut menu, click Insert Columns to the Left or Insert Columns to the Right to add a column, or Insert Rows Above or Insert Rows Below to add a row. The shortcut menu also offers Delete Rows and Delete Columns commands.

Insert a Chart

You can make complex data easier to understand by presenting that data as a chart in a slide.

A *chart* is a visual representation of numerical information. As such, charts give an instant impression of trends, tendencies, or differences, or they enable you to compare sets of data, such as sales growth over a several-year span. In PowerPoint, you can easily insert a chart by choosing the chart type and then typing your data in an Excel worksheet. The worksheet is a temporary area where you enter the chart data. You do not need to save the worksheet data as a separate file.

INSERT THE CHART

① On a slide with a content placeholder, click the Insert Chart icon.

The Create Chart dialog box appears.

② Click a chart type in the list at the left.

③ Click a specific chart type's thumbnail.

④ Click OK.

The chart appears, with placeholder data in a separate window.

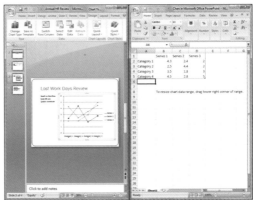

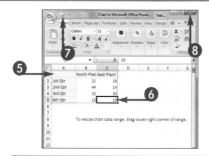

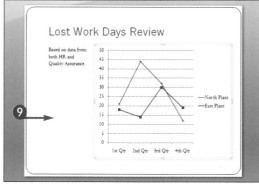

ENTER CHART DATA

⑤ Click in cells in row 1 and column A and type column labels and row labels.

Replace placeholder contents as needed, and delete any cells holding unnecessary placeholder entries.

⑥ Click in data cells below and beside the row and column headings, and type values.

⑦ Click the Update button.

You can also press Ctrl+S. If you hear a beep, your data has been saved.

⑧ Click Close.

The spreadsheet window closes, and the chart appears on the slide.

⑨ Click outside the chart to finish it.

Customize It!

After you create a chart, you can format the chart elements and change the chart data. Double-click a chart to open it for editing. Right-click various elements in the chart, such as bars in a bar chart or the chart background area. In the shortcut menu that appears, click Format (item name). You can use the dialog box that appears to change formatting. After you double-click the chart, click the Show Data button in the Data group of the Chart Tools tab to reopen the worksheet to edit chart data.

You can illustrate and enhance your presentation message using graphics such as pictures and clip art. Although the drawing tools that come with Office are handy for creating simple graphics effects, a more ambitious image requires a dedicated graphics program. With these programs, you can create professional-quality graphics and then import them into your Office document. You can also insert digital camera shots or scanned images.

If you do not have the time or the skill to create your own images, consider using clip art graphics. Clip art is professional-quality artwork that can often add just the right touch to a newsletter, brochure, or presentation. Microsoft Office ships with hundreds of clip art images in dozens of different categories, from Agriculture and Animals to Weather and Web Elements, and more clip art is available from Microsoft Office Online.

① With a slide containing a content placeholder displayed, click the Insert Picture icon.

The Insert Picture dialog box appears.

② Click the folder that contains the picture file.

You can use the Address bar, Favorite Links list, or Folders list to navigate the folders on your computer.

③ Click the picture file.

④ Click Insert.

- The selected picture is inserted into the placeholder.

⑤ With a slide containing a content placeholder displayed, click the Insert Clip Art icon.

  The Clip Art task pane appears.

⑥ Type a term to search for a clip art image to fit your presentation.

  This example uses the term *people*.

⑦ Click Go.

  Clip art graphics matching the search term appear.

⑧ Click a picture to select it.

- PowerPoint inserts the clip art.

Note: You may need to resize the clip art as desired. See "Move and Resize Objects" in Chapter 5 to learn how.

⑨ Click the Close button to close the Clip Art task pane.

Try This!
If you use a particular image regularly in your presentations, you can add it to the available clip art by importing the picture into the Clip Organizer. With the Clip Art task pane open, click Organize clips. Use the File, Add Clips to Organizer, On My Own command to locate the picture on your hard drive or removable media and add it to the Clip Organizer.

Insert Media Clips

You can add some visual or aural pizzazz to a presentation by inserting one or more media clips that play back during the slide show.

Media clips include both movie and animation clips that you can play automatically or manually during an onscreen slide show. For sounds, PowerPoint supports several file formats, including AIFF (.aiff), AU (.au), MIDI (.midi), MP3 (.mp3), Windows Audio File (.wav), and Windows Media Audio File (.wma). For animations, PowerPoint supports four file formats: Windows Media File (.asf), Windows Video File (.avi), MPEG (.mpg), and Windows Media Video File (.wmv).

Insert Media Clips

① With a slide containing a content placeholder displayed, click the Insert Media Clip icon.

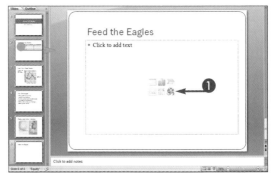

The Insert Movie dialog box appears.

② Open the folder containing the movie or sound file.

You can use the Address bar, Favorite Links list, or Folders list to navigate the folders on your computer.

③ Click a movie or sound file to insert.

④ Click OK.

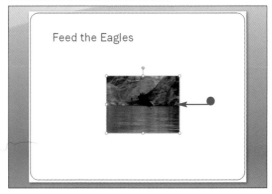

A dialog box appears asking how you want to start the media clip when you run a show.

● You can click Automatically to play the media when the slide appears.

● You can click When Clicked to play the sound when you click an icon that appears on the slide.

● The clip, or an icon for the clip, appears on the slide.

Note: *Click the Preview button on the contextual Ribbon tab that appears to preview the clip.*

Note: *Sounds that play back during a presentation are also considered media clips. To add a sound, click the Insert tab, and then click the Sound button.*

More Options!
If you want to look for media clips to insert, click the Clip Art button in the content placeholder, instead, to open the Clip Art task pane. Perform a search as you learned earlier, and optionally use the Results should be drop-down list to find only Movies (animations in the case of clip art) and/or Sounds.

Insert a SmartArt Graphic

You can insert a new SmartArt graphic or diagram to illustrate a process or structure.

Office 2007 has many new features, but one of the most impressive is support for the new SmartArt format, which is based on the XML (eXtensible Markup Language) standard. A SmartArt graphic combines text, predefined shapes, and in some cases arrows and images into a diagram. There are seven SmartArt categories: List, Process, Cycle, Hierarchy, Relationship, Matrix, and Pyramid.

For example, a diagram can show workflow in a procedure or the hierarchy in an organization. PowerPoint offers dozens of layouts for SmartArt Graphics.

---

① With a slide containing a content placeholder, click the Insert SmartArt Graphic icon.

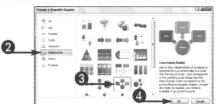

The Choose a SmartArt Graphic dialog box appears.

② Click a diagram style.

③ Click a specific diagram layout.

④ Click OK.

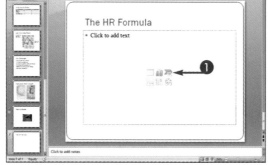

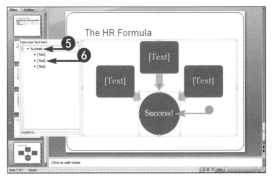

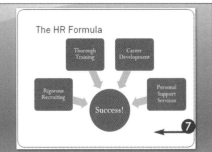

The dialog box closes, and the diagram appears on the slide ready for editing.

⑤ Type the text for the first element of the diagram.

● The text appears on the diagram.

⑥ Click in other lines of the Type your text here window and type text for other elements.

⑦ Click outside the diagram to finish creating it.

Did You Know?

The text you enter into a SmartArt Graphic will not overflow the element in which you type it. PowerPoint automatically resizes the text to fit the diagram. Note, however, that the more text you type, the smaller its size will be. Instead of adding more text to an element, you can also add more elements. In the Type your text here window, press Enter after typing the last line of text to add additional elements into the diagram.

To ensure that each slide looks exactly the way you prefer, you can edit any slide object.

When you add an object to a slide, particularly a relatively complex object such as a SmartArt Graphic, the result may not be exactly what you want. For example, a table may have incorrect or incomplete data, you may want to use a different chart type, or you may want to convert a SmartArt Graphic to a different layout. Whatever the object type, after you create an object such as a table, chart, or diagram on a slide, you can change its look and contents at any time. For example, you can change a SmartArt Graphic to a different layout, or edit the text or data in a table or chart.

① In Normal view, click the slide with the object to change in the Slides tab.

② Click the object to edit on the slide.

 PowerPoint selects the object, and displays contextual tabs for editing the object on the Ribbon.

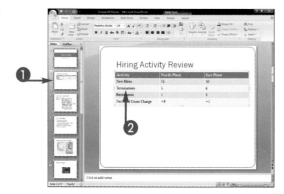

③ Edit text or data.

 For a table, click in a cell and make changes.

 For a SmartArt Graphic, edit entries in the Type your text here window.

 For a chart, click the Design tab, and click Show Data. Make changes and close the Excel window.

Note: *Working with all these slide elements is discussed earlier in this chapter.*

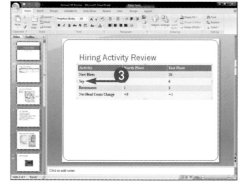

④ Use the choices on the contextual tabs that appear to make design and formatting changes.

● For example, click the Design tab (under Table Tools), and then click another style to change a table.

For a SmartArt Graphic, the Design tab under SmartArt Tools offers other Layouts and Quick Styles.

For a chart, the Design tab under Chart tools offers Chart Layouts and Chart Styles, as well as the option to change Chart Type.

⑤ Click outside the diagram to finish creating it.

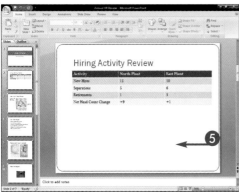

Did You Know?

Microsoft Office programs now include a Mini toolbar that pops up with helpful buttons. For example, when you select text in a table cell or SmartArt element, the Mini toolbar appears automatically and offers buttons for changing the text formatting. Move the mouse pointer over the Mini toolbar to keep it in view.

Insert a Slide from Another File

You can insert a slide from one presentation file into another. This can be a great timesaver when you have created a slide with a highly detailed chart, table, or diagram because it saves you the trouble of re-entering data and reformatting the object on the slide.

One of the secrets of PowerPoint productivity is to avoid redoing work you have performed in the past. If you have a slide with boilerplate legal disclaimer text, why re-create it in each presentation? Similarly, if you create an organization chart slide and your organization has not changed, you do not need to build the chart from scratch every time you want to add it to a presentation. For these and similar scenarios, PowerPoint enables you to reuse a slide from an existing presentation.

---

① In either Normal or Slide Sorter view, select the slide after which you want to insert the new slide.

② Click the Home tab.

③ Click the bottom portion of the New Slide button.

The layout gallery appears.

④ Click Reuse Slides.

The Reuse Slides task pane appears.

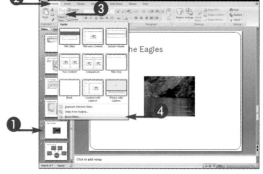

⑤ Click Open a PowerPoint File.

The Browse dialog box opens.

⑥ Open the folder containing the presentation file that contains the slide you want to insert.

⑦ Click the presentation file.

⑧ Click Open.

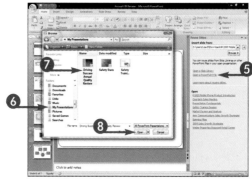

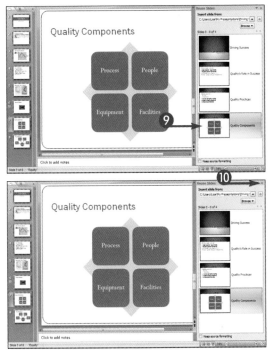

⑨ Click the slide to insert in the Reuse Slides task pane.

The slide appears in the presentation, changing to match the design used in the presentation.

⑩ Click Close to close the Reuse Slides pane.

Did You Know?

When you look at the slides in the Reuse Slides task pane, you may find it difficult to tell what they say. To get a better look, move the mouse pointer over the slide thumbnail (rather than the slide title), and an enlarged thumbnail will pop up to provide enhanced visibility and readability.

Using Themes

Themes – also called Office Document Themes – apply various types of formatting to make your slides look attractive.

By default, each new presentation you create uses a blank design theme. When you choose another theme, it applies specific colors, fonts, and placeholder positions to the slides in the presentation. The theme also can include a background color (perhaps combined with a background graphic), graphic elements such as a picture or bars and lines, and effects applied to graphics.

You can apply a theme to a single slide or the entire presentation. Generally it is better to use one theme for an entire presentation so that the elements of all slides have a consistent look and feel. However, occasionally you might choose to apply a complementary theme to a slide for emphasis.

A theme controls several design aspects of your slides. The theme determines where PowerPoint positions placeholders, the font and font size (font theme), the color theme, and the slide background.

Although slide themes provide professionally designed formats that usually work just fine out of the box, you can put your own stamp on a theme. You can change the background color or apply a different background. You also can change the color theme or font theme.

Quick Tips

If you want to apply a particular design to just a few slides, you can select those slides and apply a theme.

If your presentation includes several distinct sections, you may not want to apply the same design to every slide. Instead, you might want to make each section stand out by applying a different theme to each section. PowerPoint

normally applies a theme to the entire presentation. However, you can apply a different theme to the currently selected slide or slides in either Normal or Slide Sorter view. If you apply a different theme to a single slide, be sure it complements the design used on other slides. The transition from one theme to another as you move from slide to slide can be jarring to your viewers.

① Select the slide(s) to format in Normal or Slide Sorter view.

Note: *After selecting the first slide in the Slides tab or Slide Sorter view, Ctrl+click thumbnails to select additional slides.*

② Click the Design tab.

③ Click the More button.

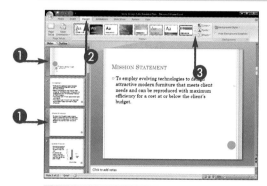

The gallery of themes appears.

④ Move your mouse pointer to a theme thumbnail.

● PowerPoint's Live Preview feature previews the new design in the Slide pane.

You can scroll down the gallery to view additional themes, if available.

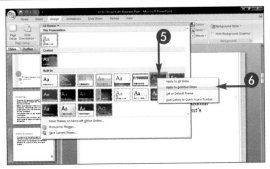

⑤ When you find the theme to apply, right-click its thumbnail.

⑥ Click Apply to Selected Slides.

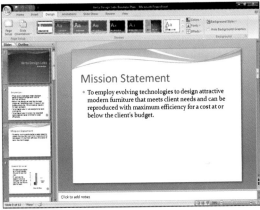

PowerPoint applies the theme to the slides you selected.

Did You Know?

When applying themes, remember that, in general, darker backgrounds with light-colored text work better in a darker space, such as a hotel conference room. Similarly, lighter backgrounds are easier to read in a brighter, smaller space, such as a small meeting room. Also, note that people may grow weary from looking at bright colors such as orange or red in longer presentations.

You can give your entire presentation a consistent, professional appearance by applying a theme to all the slides in the presentation.

One of the cardinal rules of presentation design is to avoid anything that will distract your audience from the message you are trying to convey. If you apply many different designs to your slides, the jarring transition from one design to another is bound to become just such a

distraction. It is almost always best to apply one theme to all the slides in a presentation. This gives your slides a consistent look, and because PowerPoint's themes are designed by graphic artists, they give your presentation a professional appearance. While the layouts may vary, the theme supplies common colors, fonts, and more so that you can focus on content rather than design and formatting.

① Click the Design tab.

② Click More.

   The gallery of themes appears.

③ Move your mouse pointer to a theme thumbnail.

   PowerPoint's Live Preview feature previews the new design in the Slide pane.

④ Click the thumbnail of the theme you want to apply.

● PowerPoint applies the theme to all the slides in the presentation.

   You also can right-click a thumbnail in the gallery and then click Apply to All Slides.

VERTA DESIGN LABS

You can choose from a wide variety of themes by searching for themes on the Microsoft Office Online Web site.

PowerPoint comes with about 20 themes installed, and these predefined themes are professionally designed and attractive. However, sometimes you may want a change of pace. You learn later in this chapter how to customize these themes.

If you do not have the time to do that, you can also examine a wide variety of themes that Microsoft makes available on the Web. You can download these themes from the Microsoft Office Online Web site. This site enables you to search for themes and templates by program or keyword.

① Click the Design tab.

② Click More.

③ Click More Themes on Microsoft Office Online.

The Microsoft Office Online site opens in your browser.

You must have an Internet connection available to reach this site.

④ Type in a search term.

⑤ Click Search.

A list of templates appears.

⑥ Click a template.

A page with information about the template appears.

⑦ Click Download Now.

Messages may appear to prompt you to install an ActiveX control or allow an action to continue. Respond to the messages as needed.

The theme appears in PowerPoint, applied to a new presentation.

Each document theme includes a color theme. You can add variety or emphasize a particular slide by applying another color theme to individual slides.

If the colors that come with a predefined theme are not quite what you want, you can change them individually. However, if you want to avoid the drudgery of getting your text, line, background, and fill colors to match, PowerPoint comes with more

than 20 built-in color schemes that do the hard work for you. Each color scheme has eight color swatches: The first is the background color, the second is the text color, and the rest are accent colors that PowerPoint uses with content such as charts and SmartArt diagrams. You can apply a new color theme to one or more slides in Normal view or Slide Sorter view.

---

① Select the slide(s) to format in the Slides tab of Normal or Slide Sorter view, using Ctrl+click if needed.

② Click the Design tab.

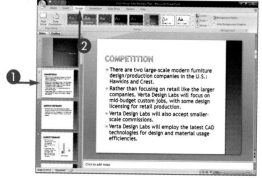

③ Click Colors.

④ Right-click the desired theme.

⑤ Click Apply to Selected Slides.

● The color theme appears on selected slides.

Moving the mouse pointer over a color theme previews the theme in the Slide pane.

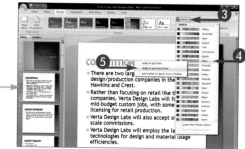

You can apply a new color theme to all the slides in a presentation. Doing so can give a whole new look and feel to the overall document theme, while retaining the theme's other attributes.

After you apply a theme, you may find that you do not like the colors used in the theme. If you like the other theme elements — such as the fonts and background — you might not want to change the theme entirely. In that case, PowerPoint enables you to change just the theme colors, which means you can preserve the other theme elements.

Changing the color theme also can help you get more attractive results when displaying the slide show or printing the presentation.

① Click the Design tab.

② Click Colors.

③ Click the desired theme.

Moving the mouse pointer over a color theme previews the theme in the Slide pane.

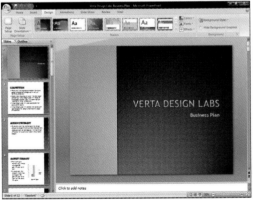

PowerPoint applies the color theme to the entire presentation.

To create your own custom color theme, click Colors, and then click Create New Theme Colors. Select colors, type a name in the Create New Theme Colors dialog box, and then click Save. You can then apply the theme as needed.

You can enhance the look of your presentation or make your presentation text more readable by applying a different font theme.

Note that each theme defines two fonts: a larger font for title text and a smaller font for body text. The typeface is usually the same for both types of text, but some themes use two different typefaces, such as Arial for titles and Times New Roman for body text. You can change the font theme for the entire presentation if you prefer to use alternate fonts that are more suitable for your presentation.

You cannot change the font theme for individual slides. PowerPoint always applies the font to all the slides in the presentation.

---

1 Click the Design tab.

2 Click the Fonts button.

3 Click a theme.

Moving the mouse pointer over a font theme previews the theme in the Slide pane.

● PowerPoint applies the font theme to the entire presentation.

To create your own custom font theme, click Fonts, and then click Create New Theme Fonts. Select fonts and enter a name in the Create New Theme Fonts dialog box, and then click Save. You can then apply the theme as needed.

You can spruce up your slides by applying a different background to some or all of the slides. The document theme applies a background (sometimes plain white) on which all slide elements sit. You can change the background for one slide or all of them to update the presentation's look.

For example, though a plain white background may work best for printing,

you may prefer to add a subtle background color for slide show playback.

For each theme, PowerPoint offers a dozen different background styles. The background styles you see depend on the overall theme you have chosen. In each case, PowerPoint offers background styles that complement the other colors in the theme.

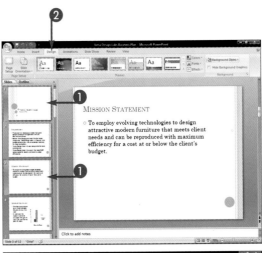

① Select the slide(s) to format in the Slides tab in Normal or Slide Sorter view, using Ctrl+click if needed.

You can skip this step if you want to change the background for all slides.

② Click the Design tab.

③ Click Background Styles.

④ Right-click the desired theme.

Moving the mouse pointer over a font theme previews the theme in the Slide pane.

⑤ Click Apply to All Slides, or if you selected slides in step 1, Apply to Selected Slides.

PowerPoint applies the background to the selected slides or the entire presentation.

If you want to apply the background to all the slides, you can skip steps **4** and **5** and simply click the desired background style.

Apply a Texture or Picture Background

You can push design limits even further by using either a texture or a digital picture as a background.

Most themes offer a solid color background, which is usually a good choice because you do not want your background to interfere with the slide content. However, each theme not only gives you a choice of background colors, but it also gives you your choice of fill effects, such as pictures

or textures. For example, you can use a digital photo of a new product as the background for a new product presentation.

You can apply the texture or picture background to selected slides or the whole presentation. Note, too, that PowerPoint automatically adjusts the text color if you choose a darker or lighter background color.

APPLY A TEXTURE BACKGROUND

① Select the slide(s) to format in the Slides tab of Normal or Slide Sorter view.

② Click the Design tab.

③ Click Background Styles.

④ Click Format Background.

The Format Background dialog box appears.

⑤ Click the Picture or texture fill option.

⑥ Click the Texture button.

PowerPoint displays a texture gallery.

⑦ Click a texture.

⑧ Finish applying the background.

If you selected slides in step 1, click Close.

To apply the background to all slides, click Apply to All before clicking Close.

The new background appears.

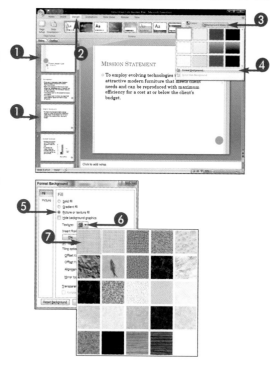

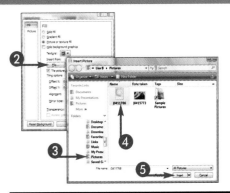

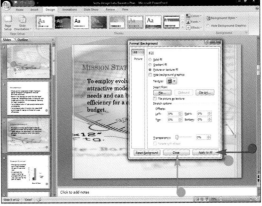

APPLY A PICTURE BACKGROUND

1 Perform steps **1** to **5** on the previous page.

2 Click File.

The Insert Picture dialog box appears.

3 Navigate to the folder that contains the desired picture file.

4 Click the picture file.

5 Click Insert.

The Insert Picture dialog box closes.

6 Finish applying the background.

● If you selected slides in step 1, click Close to apply the background to those slides only.

● To apply the background to all slides in the presentation, click Apply to All before clicking Close.

The new background appears where specified.

Did You Know?

When you are deciding which kinds of backgrounds work best in presentations, you can follow the same guidelines as for selecting themes. Darker backgrounds with lighter text work well for onscreen presentations, and lighter backgrounds with darker text work best for printed materials. Choose patterns and images that are small or subtle so that the text remains readable.

If you applied a color theme, font theme, and background that really work together, you can save that combination as a new document theme that you can apply to other presentations.

If you go to the trouble of choosing a theme and then customizing that scheme with custom colors, different fonts, a new background, and perhaps also a background texture or picture, you probably do not want to go through the entire process the next time you want the same theme for a presentation. Fortunately, you do not have to because PowerPoint enables you to save all of your theme details as a custom theme.

---

① Click the Design tab.

② Click More.

   The gallery of themes appears.

③ Click Save Current Theme.

   The Save Current Theme dialog box appears.

④ Type a file name.

   There is no need to change the save folder. Using the default location ensures that the custom theme will show up in the gallery of themes.

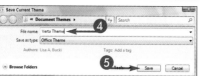

⑤ Click Save.

   PowerPoint adds the theme to the gallery in a special section labeled Custom.

You can most easily apply a theme that you use regularly by making that theme the default PowerPoint theme for new presentations.

The default theme is the one that PowerPoint automatically applies to every new presentation. The standard default theme applies to each new presentation a blank background as well as the Calibri font in varying sizes depending on the placeholder. You may find that you constantly change this standard theme to some other theme. Although it is easy to change themes at any time, you can save time by configuring PowerPoint to use that theme as the default for all new presentations.

1. Click the Design tab.
2. Click More.

   The gallery of themes appears.

3. Right-click the theme to set as the default.
4. Click Set as Default Theme.

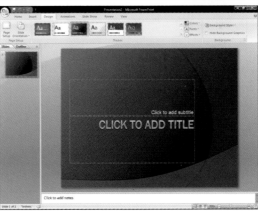

The theme immediately becomes the default theme. Any blank presentation you create will use that theme.

To return to the original default theme, perform steps **1** to **4** to set the Office Theme as the default. If you point to a theme in the gallery, a ScreenTip with the theme name pops up.

If you have a theme as well as presentation content that you want to reuse in other presentations, you can save time by saving the theme and content as a template file.

A *template* is a file upon which you base a new document. In PowerPoint, a template includes both the presentation design and

reusable template content, such as bulleted lists you use often in a sales presentation. You can save any presentation as a template so that you can create new presentations using the template's formatting and contents.

① Click Office.

② Click Save As.

Make sure to click the button graphic and not the right arrow.

The Save As dialog box appears.

③ Type a file name.

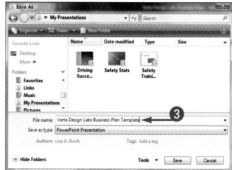

④ Click here and select PowerPoint Template.

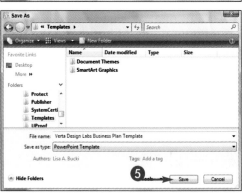

The Save in folder changes to Templates.

⑤ Click Save.

The presentation is saved as a template. Use it by double-clicking My Templates in the New Presentation dialog box.

Check It Out!

There are many templates on Microsoft Office Online Web site that you might consider downloading. Also, many people and companies make PowerPoint templates available online. Some of them are free, and others will cost you. A few sites to explore are www.animationfactory. com and www.presentationcafe.com. You can also type the phrase "PowerPoint templates" in your favorite search engine to find others.

Using Masters

Masters enable you to make global settings for your slides, such as inserting your company logo or a page number on every slide.

PowerPoint offers three master views. Each enables you to set up the basic infrastructure for your slides to save you from having to arrange and design elements on every slide.

PowerPoint uses the Slide Master, Handout Master, and Notes Master to control page layouts. Slide Master consists of an overall theme master and a master for each slide layout. PowerPoint applies changes made to placeholders, the background, and graphics on a master to corresponding presentation slides. Handout Master

controls the layout of printed handouts, and Notes Master controls how printed Notes pages look.

When you make a change, such as increasing the font size for slide titles or adding a footer or graphic on a master, PowerPoint applies that change to every slide in the presentation. This saves you time and gives your presentation a consistent look and feel.

When you make changes to individual slides — for example, changing the font in Normal view — that change takes precedence over master settings. You also can omit any graphics you have placed on Slide Master using the Background group on the Design tab of the Ribbon.

Quick Tips

Display and Close Slide Master View

You can work with the Slide Master by switching to the Slide Master view via PowerPoint's View tab. Opening Slide Master view automatically displays tabs for working with the master.

After you change the Slide Master and close the view, PowerPoint redisplays whatever view you had open previously — either Normal view or Slide Sorter view. Your global changes appear there.

When you apply a document theme to your presentation, PowerPoint automatically creates a set of slide masters containing all the settings for that theme. If you go to Slide Master view and make changes, you can then save a new theme, which will preserve the new master. If you apply more than one slide design to your presentation, you can create multiple master sets.

① Click the View tab.

② Click Slide Master.

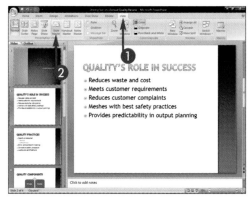

Slide Master view and the Ribbon tabs for working with masters appear.

③ Click the Slide Master tab, if needed.

④ To close the Slide Master view, click Close Master View.

Slide Master view closes.

To go back to a view other than the one you used previously, click the View tab and then click the desired view button in the Presentation Views group.

You can customize a particular slide layout by removing a placeholder from that layout using the Slide Master view.

The layouts in the Slide Master contain placeholders for the slide title, text or graphic content, date, footer, and slide numbers. If you are not using a particular placeholder, you may prefer to remove it from the slide layout in the master.

Note that deleting the title or text placeholder from the slide master layout at the top does not delete the title from other slide layouts. When you work with a particular layout in the Slide Master view, any changes you make apply only to that layout.

① With Slide Master view displayed, click the layout with the placeholder to remove in the left pane.

② Click the placeholder to delete.

PowerPoint selects the placeholder.

③ Right-click the border of the placeholder to delete.

A shortcut menu appears.

④ Click Cut.

The placeholder disappears.

Note: *If you delete a placeholder from a layout, the placeholder is only removed from slides already using that layout. Any content you inserted into that placeholder on a slide remains in place. Slides added to the presentation after you remove the placeholder from the master will no longer have the placeholder.*

Note: *If you delete the placeholder for footer, date, or time and then display that information, it will appear on the slide or may appear in an unexpected location.*

You can create a custom slide layout by inserting a new placeholder onto a slide layout using the Slide Master view.

You may find yourself constantly modifying one of the slide layouts by adding a particular type of object. For example, you may always add different clip art images to your slides in the lower right corner. In that case, you can save a bit of time by adding a clip art placeholder

to that slide layout using the Slide Master view. This enables you to quickly click the placeholder to add your clip art. You can insert placeholders for text and other types of content such as charts, tables, SmartArt, and media.

Note that you also can resize, reposition, or reformat any slide placeholder at any time. Click the placeholder's border to select it, and then make the desired changes.

① With Slide Master view displayed, click the slide layout where you would like to add a placeholder in the left pane.

② Click the Slide Master tab, if necessary.

③ Click the bottom portion of the Insert Placeholder button, with the down arrow.

A menu of placeholders appears.

④ Click the desired type of placeholder to insert.

Clicking the Content choice inserts a placeholder where you can click an icon to insert the specified content, as on a slide using the Title and Content layout.

⑤ Drag on the slide with the cross-hair pointer that appears to create the placeholder.

● When you release the mouse button, the placeholder appears.

⑥ With the new placeholder still selected, click either the Home or Animations tab.

⑦ Use the tools found on the tab to format the placeholder.

⑧ Click outside the placeholder when you finish.

Customize It!

To move or resize a placeholder, first click its border to select it. To move the placeholder, point to any area on the border between two handles and drag. To resize the placeholder, move the mouse pointer over one of the handles, and drag it.

Slide masters include a placeholder for footer information that you want to include on every slide, such as your company name.

In a large presentation, you can easily lose track of what slide number you are working with or viewing. Similarly, if you work with a lot of presentations, you can easily get confused as to which presentation you are currently working on. To help overcome

these and other organizational handicaps, take advantage of the footers that PowerPoint enables you to display on a presentation's slides.

By default, PowerPoint does not display the footer in each slide. (Or, more accurately, it displays a blank footer in each slide.) To display the footer, you need to activate the footer content.

---

1 In Normal, Slide Master, or another view, click the Insert tab.

The Insert tab appears at a slightly different position on the Ribbon depending on the current view.

2 Click Header & Footer.

3 Click Footer.

4 Type your footer here.

5 Click the Don't show on title slide check box to prevent the footer or other elements from displaying on the first slide in the file.

6 Click an option to apply the footer text and close the dialog box:

You can click Apply to All to add the footer to all slides.

You can click Apply to add the footer only to slide(s) selected before you started these steps.

The footer appears on slides as specified.

You can display the current date and time as part of your presentation.

By default, PowerPoint adds the date as a fixed quantity in a master; this means that the date is simply text and will not change with each presentation. You may prefer to include a date that updates automatically based on the computer's system date. To

do this, you use the Header and Footer dialog box, which you can access from any view. The Header and Footer dialog box also enables you to display just the current time (again, updated automatically from the system clock) or both the date and time.

1. Click the Insert tab.

2. Click Header & Footer.

3. Click the Date and time check box.

   The available date settings become active.

4. Click the Update automatically option.

   The Update automatically drop-down list becomes active.

5. Click here and select a date or date and time format.

6. Click an option to apply the date and close the dialog box:

   You can click Apply to All to add the date to all slides.

   You can click Apply to add the date only to any slide(s) selected before you started these steps.

   The date appears on slides as specified.

Set Up Slide Numbers

You can make your presentations easier to navigate by displaying the slide numbers.

PowerPoint keeps tracks of the slide numbers in your presentation. The slide numbers correspond to the order in which your slides appear. For example, the title slide is usually slide 1, the next slide is slide 2, and so on. If you insert a slide between existing slides, PowerPoint updates the slide numbers accordingly.

You can have PowerPoint automatically number the presentation slides and display those numbers during a slide show. You set up slide numbers using the Header and Footer dialog box. Note, too, that you can use the master views to reposition or resize the slide number placeholder.

① Click the Insert tab.

② Click Header & Footer.

③ Click the Slide number check box.

④ Click an option to apply the page numbers and close the dialog box:

   You can click Apply to All to add the page numbers to all slides.

   You can click Apply to add the page numbers only to any slide(s) selected before you started these steps.

● Page numbers appear on slides as specified.

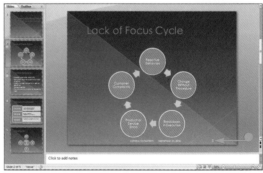

You can use the Slide Master view to insert a graphic that appears on every slide. You may find that you insert the same image in all your slides. For example, your organization or company might want its logo on all slides for professionalism and consistency. Similarly, if your presentation has a particular theme, you might want an image related to that theme to appear on all the slides.

By adding the image to the master thumbnail in the Slide Master view, PowerPoint automatically displays the image on all your slides.

Choosing the theme thumbnail ensures the inserted graphic will appear on most of the other slide layouts in a master. If the graphic does not appear on a specific slide layout, select the thumbnail for that layout master and insert the graphic again.

① With Slide Master view displayed, click the theme master thumbnail.

② Click the Insert tab.

③ Click Picture.

The Insert Picture dialog box appears.

④ Navigate to the folder that contains the picture you want to insert.

⑤ Click the graphics file you want.

⑥ Click Insert.

● The dialog box closes and the picture appears on the master, where you can move and resize it as needed.

You can work with multiple presentation themes more efficiently by creating a new, custom master in the Slide Master view.

Some of the most effective presentation designs are ones that apply a particular design to groups of related slides. For example, on a budget presentation, you might use a green color scheme on income-related slides and a red color scheme on expense-related slides. Similarly, in a presentation that includes both sensitive and nonsensitive material, you could add a "For Internal Use Only" graphic to the slides with sensitive material.

PowerPoint allows you to have more than one Slide Master in a presentation. You can then apply one of the Slide Masters to the appropriate slides, and any changes you make to that Slide Master will affect only those slides.

① With Slide Master view displayed, click the Slide Master tab.

② Click Insert Slide Master.

● A new slide master appears here.

If you click the Themes button on the Slide Master tab in Slide Master view and then right-click a theme in the gallery, you can click Add as New Slide Master to insert another master using an existing theme.

③ Make formatting changes to the master as desired.

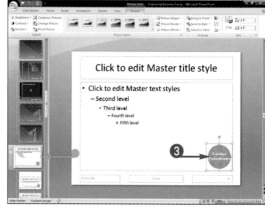

You can ensure that you can use a particular master in the future by preserving that master.

If you delete all the slides that use a particular master, PowerPoint removes the master from the presentation. This is usually the behavior you want, because it keeps the master view uncluttered.

However, this can be a problem if you think you will need to use the master again in the future. To keep the master in the file, you need to preserve it.

Keep in mind that even if it is preserved, you can still manually delete the master in Slide Master view.

① With Slide Master view displayed, click the theme master thumbnail.

If a pushpin appears with the theme master thumbnail, the master is already preserved.

② Click the Slide Master tab, if needed.

③ Click Preserve.

● PowerPoint preserves the master, and a pushpin appears on the theme master thumbnail.

● The Preserve button on the Ribbon also becomes highlighted.

To unpreserve a master, perform steps **1** and **2** again.

You can create a custom layout for your presentation's Notes pages by modifying the structure of the Notes Master.

If you use Notes pages extensively in PowerPoint, you might not find the default Notes layout ideal. For example, you might want to use a different font, or you might want to change the position of the notes. You can perform these and other customization tasks using PowerPoint's Notes Master view, which

enables you to modify the layout for printed Notes pages. This master has a placeholder for the slide and one for the Notes area, as well as header, footer, date, and slide number placeholders.

You can modify the format of notes text, move placeholders around, delete placeholders, and enter header and footer text for printed Notes pages. See Chapter 9 for information about printing Notes.

① Click the View tab.

② Click Notes Master.

The Notes Master view appears.

③ Click a placeholder border, or click within a placeholder and type text that you want to appear on notes pages.

● You can click the notes text placeholder border and then click tools on the Edit Master tab to change text formatting or font.

● You can click a placeholder border and then drag the placeholder to another location.

● You can click and type to enter header text.

● You can click and type to enter footer text.

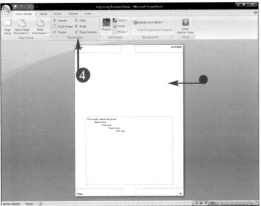

④ Click to uncheck and check items in the Placeholders group on the Notes Master tab as needed.

● Unchecked placeholders disappear from the master. Rechecking an item reinstates it on the master.

⑤ Click the Notes Master tab, if you have worked on any of the other available tabs before finishing.

⑥ Click Close Master View.

Notes Master view closes.

TIP

More Options!
If you want to enable and choose a format for date and time to be printed on Notes pages, you can use the same procedure as for setting slide date and time. When you open the Header and Footer dialog box, click the Notes and Handouts tab. Click the Date and Time check box to enable options, and then select a date and time format from the drop-down list. Click Apply to All and all your notes and handouts will use that date format.

Work with the Handout Master

You can create a custom layout for your presentation's Handout pages by modifying the structure of the Handout Master.

You use Handout pages to give your audience hard copies of the presentation. If your Handout pages are attractive and well-organized, your audience will appreciate it and give your presentation a more positive review. To that end, you can customize your Handout pages using

PowerPoint's Handout Master view, which enables you to modify the layout for printed Handout pages. This master has a header, footer, date, and slide number placeholders. You can choose a handout layout, as well as work with header and footer placeholders to control the appearance of your printed handouts. You also can use choices on the other tabs in Handout Master view to adjust handout appearance.

① Click the View tab.

② Click Handout Master.

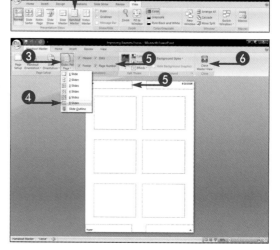

Handout Master View appears.

③ On the Handout Master tab, click Slides per page.

④ Click another layout.

The preview changes to the new layout.

⑤ Work with placeholders as desired.

⑥ Click Close Master View.

Handout Master view closes.

You can control your master graphics by removing them from any slides where they are not appropriate,

Earlier in this chapter you saw how to insert a graphic in the Slide Master view's master thumbnail. When you do this, PowerPoint displays the image on every slide in your presentation. Ideally, you then compose your slides to work around

this image because the image and your other slide content should never overlap. However, you may have a particularly full slide that contains a great deal of content. If the master graphic overlaps or interferes with your slide content, PowerPoint enables you to override the master graphic and hide on that slide.

① In Normal view, click the Design tab.

② Click Hide Background Graphics.

● A check mark appears beside the option, and the master graphics disappear from the slide.

You can create a custom slide master by adding a custom slide layout. Earlier you saw that you can create an entire new slide master to customize. However, if you require just a different slide layout, creating an entire slide master is overkill. Instead, you can work in the Slide Master view to add a new slide layout to the current master. You can then customize that layout to get the effect you require.

For example, you want to create a slide layout with three content placeholders. You can do so in Slide Master view, and then PowerPoint makes that layout available so that you can apply it to slides in your presentation.

① Click the View tab.

② Click Slide Master.

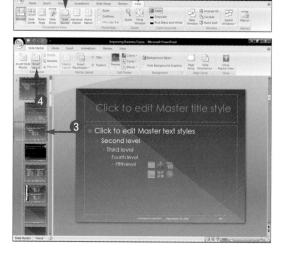

The Slide Master view appears.

③ If optional, click the thumbnail for the layout below which you want to insert the new slide layout.

④ Click Insert Layout.

The new custom layout appears in the pane at the left, selected so that you can edit it.

5 Use available tools such as the Insert Placeholder button to create and format the elements in your slide layout.

6 Click Close Master View.

Add slides using your custom slide layout to the presentation as needed.

7 Click the Home tab.

8 Click the New Slide button.

9 Click your custom layout.

More Options!

You can assign a unique name to your custom slide layout. In Slide Master view, right-click the layout thumbnail in the left pane, and then click Rename Layout. Type the name you want in the Rename Layout dialog box, and then click Rename.

Adding Graphics and Drawings

When most people think about using the Office programs, they generally think about text, whether it is writing sentences and paragraphs in Word, adding formulas and labels in Excel, creating slide titles and bullets in PowerPoint, and so on. It is certainly true that most of the work people do in Office – from papers to purchase orders to presentations – is and should remain text-based.

However, if you *only* think text when you think of Office, you are missing out on a whole other dimension. The main Office 2007 programs – Word, Excel, PowerPoint, and Outlook – have extensive new graphics

tools that you can take advantage of to improve the clarity of your work or just to add a bit of visual interest to liven up an otherwise drab document.

For PowerPoint in particular, adding graphic elements such as photographs, WordArt, and shapes to your slides can enhance the attractiveness and effectiveness of your presentation. You can place graphic elements anywhere on a slide; you are not bound by placeholders on the slide layout. You can also use color and various formatting options to make your presentation picture-perfect.

Quick Tips

If you do not have the time or the artistic skill to create your own images, you can use clip art graphics, instead. Clip art is professional-quality artwork that can often add just the right touch to a presentation. Microsoft Office ships with hundreds of clip art images in dozens of different categories, from Agriculture and Animals to Weather and Web Elements.

PowerPoint offers clip art in the form of picture, illustration, sound, and movie (animation) files. You can search for clip art by keyword or phrase and can even find clip art online. Once you find and select a clip art graphic, you can insert it anywhere on your slide — without using an existing content placeholder.

① With the slide you want to insert the clip art into displayed in Normal view, click the Insert tab.

② Click the Clip Art button.

The Clip Art task pane appears.

③ Type a search term.

If you want to search particular collections or only locations on your system's hard disk, open the Search in drop-down list and choose the collections to search. The Everywhere choice automatically searches for clips online.

④ Click Go.

Search results appear.

● Any clip found on the Web has a small globe icon in the lower-left corner of the thumbnail.

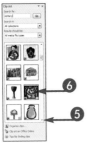

⑤ Scroll to locate the clip you want.

⑥ Click the clip.

● PowerPoint inserts the clip on your slide.

Note: See the section "Move and Resize Objects" to learn how to change the clip's size and position.

● A clip with a star icon in the lower-left corner also includes animation. Such a clip prints like an illustration, but includes motion during slide show playback.

● Tools for formatting the clip art also appear on the Ribbon.

⑦ Click Close.

The Clip Art task pane closes.

Try This!

You can also insert a clip from the Microsoft Office Online site. After you display the Clip Art task pane, click the Clip art on Office Online link. The Web browser launches and displays the Clip Art page for Microsoft Office Online so that you can search for and download clips.

Insert an Image File

You can add visual interest to a slide by inserting an image file that is stored on your computer.

A typical PowerPoint presentation consists of mostly text: titles, subtitles, bullets, and so on. You can keep your audience's attention by occasionally inserting an image into a slide. For example, you could put your company logo on the title page.

Similarly, if your presentation discusses a product, you could include a picture of that product.

After you insert an image file, it becomes an object on your slide. You can then move, resize, and format it. Later sections provide more information about formatting picture files.

① With the slide you want to insert the image on displayed in Normal view, click the Insert tab.

② Click the Picture button.

The Insert Picture dialog box appears.

③ Select a folder to look in, if necessary.

④ Click the image file you want to insert.

⑤ Click Insert.

● The image appears on your slide.

You can enhance the look of a slide by drawing a predefined shape such as a star or arrow.

A *shape* is an object such as a line or rectangle that you draw within your slide. You can use shapes to point out key features in a presentation, enclose text, create flowcharts, and enhance the look of a slide. In PowerPoint 2007, you can use seven shape types: Lines (straight lines, squiggles, freeform polygons, arrows, connectors, and curves); Basic Shapes (rectangles, triangles, circles, boxes, cylinders, hearts, and many more); Block Arrows (two-dimensional arrows of various configurations); Flowchart (the standard shapes used for creating flowcharts); Callouts (boxes and lines for creating callouts to slide features); Stars and Banners (stars, starbursts, scrolls, and more); and Action Buttons (buttons such as forward and backward that represent standard slide show actions; see Chapter 7).

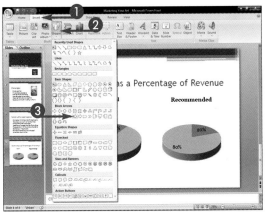

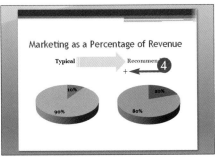

① With the slide where you want to insert a shape in displayed in Normal view, click the Insert tab.

② Click the Shapes button.

The gallery of available shapes, organized by category, appears.

③ Click the button for the shape to draw.

If you point to a shape button, a pop-up tip will show you the shape's name.

The gallery closes, and the mouse pointer changes to a crosshair (+).

④ Drag diagonally on the slide to draw the shape.

To draw a perfect square or circle when you are using the Rectangle or Oval shape, press and hold the Shift key as you drag. When you release the mouse button, the shape appears.

Add a Text Box

You can add a text box that behaves like a slide layout placeholder anywhere on a slide.

The graphics you add to your documents will usually consist of images, but times will occur when you need to augment those images with some text. For example, you may want to add a title and subtitle or insert a label. To add text to an existing image, you draw a text box and then type your text within that box. The text box automatically enlarges or shrinks and wraps to more lines within the box depending on the amount of text you type. Keep in mind that text box contents do not appear in your presentation outline.

---

① With the slide you want to add a text box to displayed in Normal view, click the Insert tab.

② Click the Text Box button.

The mouse pointer changes to an upside-down cross.

③ Drag diagonally on the slide to draw the box.

The mouse pointer changes to a crosshair (+) as you drag.

Dragging primarily establishes the box width. The height adjusts automatically based on the amount of text you type.

The text box appears with an insertion point inside.

④ Type your text.

⑤ Click anywhere outside the text box to deselect it.

The text appears on your slide.

If you think that a plain text box lacks excitement, you can create a jazzier text box by adding text to a shape you have already drawn.

The text placeholders that appear on PowerPoint's slide layouts are always rectangular boxes. Similarly, any text boxes that you insert by hand will also have a rectangular shape. That is fine for most situations, but you can create visual interest by adding text to a nonrectangular shape. In particular, you can add text to another object on the slide. You can do this with shapes, pictures, clip art, or a chart. The text appears within the shape, and the shape effectively becomes a text box.

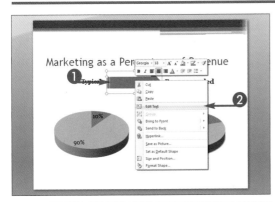

① Right-click the shape in which you want to add text.

② Click Edit Text.

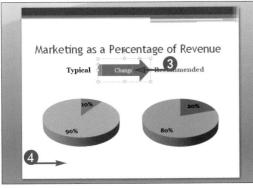

The insertion point appears inside the shape.

③ Type your text.

④ Click anywhere outside the shape to deselect it.

The text appears in the shape.

To change object contents, formatting, size, or position, you first must select the object to change. Selecting an object tells PowerPoint to display the tools for formatting the object on the Ribbon, and to apply your changes to the selected object only.

Every graphic object has an invisible rectangular frame. For a line or rectangle, the frame is the same as the object itself. For all other objects, the frame is a rectangle that completely encloses the shape or image. Before you can format or edit a graphic object, you must select it, which displays selection handles around the frame.

The method for selecting an object varies slightly depending on the type of object.

① With the slide that has the object to select displayed in Normal view, click the object.

Clicking a text box once displays the insertion point for editing. Clicking the selection box again selects it for formatting, changing its outline to a solid line. After you click a chart, click again to select an individual element such as the legend.

② To select multiple objects on the slide, click the Home tab.

③ Click Select.

④ Click Select All.

Alternatively, you can Shift+click on additional objects to select them.

You can press Ctrl+A to select all slide objects.

● Additional selection boxes appear.

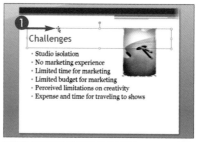

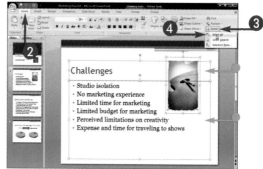

You can enhance the look of your graphics by applying one or more effects.

When you select an object, you can use a Ribbon button to apply various effects to the object. You can use these effects to add more dimension and realism to the object's appearance.

The Shadow effects apply drop shadows to the object to enhance depth; the

Reflection effects display a copy of the object that looks like a reflection of the object on a smooth surface; the Glow effects display a fuzzy border around to object that makes the object appear to be glowing; the Soft Edges effects blend the edges of the object with the slide background; and the 3-D Rotation effects rotate the object in the third dimension.

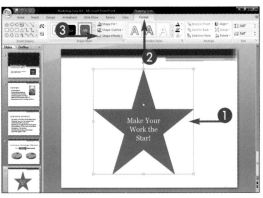

① In Normal view, select the object to format.

② Click the Format tab.

③ Click the appropriate effects button: Shape Effects if you selected an object, text box, or chart; or Picture Effects if you selected a clip art or picture object.

Note: *The Format tab's tools vary depending on the object you selected in step 1.*

④ Point to a type of effect on the menu that appears.

A submenu or gallery of more specific choices appears.

⑤ Move the mouse pointer over one of the choices.

A preview of that effect appears on the object.

⑥ Click the desired effect.

PowerPoint applies the effect to the object.

Format Objects

You can adjust the formatting of an object to make it more visually appealing or easier to see against the slide background.

All objects come with a wide array of formatting options, so if you do not like the look of an object, you can apply one or more of these formats. For example, you can change the object's *fill*, which is

the area inside the edges of the image. The fill is usually white, but you can format the fill with a solid color, a color gradient, a picture, or a texture.

For outlines and line shapes, you can change the thickness, style (say, for solid to dashed), and color. You can also add or remove arrows if the image is a line shape.

---

① Right-click the object to format on the slide.

② Click the appropriate choice in the menu that appears: Format Shape or Format Picture.

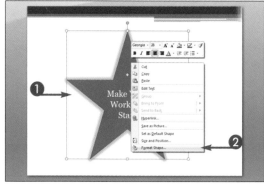

The Format Shape or Format Picture dialog box appears.

● Leave the Solid fill option selected.

③ Click the Color button.

A color palette appears.

④ Click the color with which to fill the object.

After you click a color, drag the Transparency slider as desired to make the object fill more or less transparent.

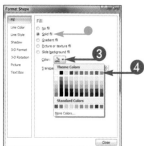

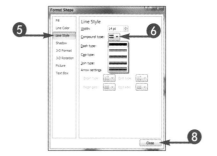

⑤ Click another item in the list at the left to display formatting choices for that type of item in the dialog box.

The type of object selected in step 1 determines which formatting settings are available.

⑥ Change the detailed settings for the selected formatting item as desired.

⑦ Repeat steps **5** and **6** to change other formatting settings as desired.

⑧ Click Close.

● PowerPoint applies the formatting changes to the object.

The Format tab of the Ribbon offers a variety of choices for changing object formatting.

Did You Know?

You can configure an object so that PowerPoint always applies a particular format when you insert that object. Draw any shape and then use the Format Shape dialog box to select the fill color and line style you want to use. Then right-click the shape and click Set as Default Shape.

Move and Resize Objects

You can resize and reposition the object to fit better on your slide.

When you use your mouse to click-and-drag an object onto a slide, it's not always easy to get the object's dimensions and position just right the first time. If a graphic is too large or too small for your needs, or if the object's shape is not what you want, you can resize the image to change its dimensions or its shape. Similarly, if a graphic is not in the position you want within the slide, you can move the object to a different part of the slide.

When you select an object, handles appear on the selection box. Drag a handle to resize an object. Dragging a corner handle retains the object's original proportions.

MOVE OBJECTS

① Select the object to move.

The mouse pointer changes to a four-headed arrow pointer when you move it over a selected object.

② Drag the object to a new position.

When you release the mouse button, the object appears in its new position.

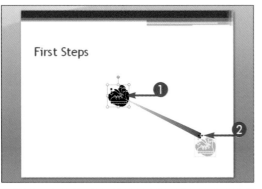

RESIZE OBJECTS

① Select the object to resize.

Handles appear around it.

② Drag a handle outward (from the object's center) to enlarge it or inward to shrink it.

When you release the mouse button, the object appears at its new size.

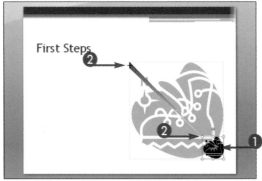

You can give an object a more dynamic look by rotating the object or flipping it.

Most graphic objects get inserted into a document without any rotation: Horizontal borders appear horizontal, and vertical borders appear vertical. A nonrotated image is probably what you will want most of the time, but for some occasions an image tilted at a jaunty angle

is just the right touch for a slide. Many objects come with a rotation handle that you can use to rotate the object clockwise or counterclockwise. PowerPoint also enables you to quickly flip an object horizontally or vertically. The Format tab offers the flip and rotation tools. You also can drag to freely rotate an object.

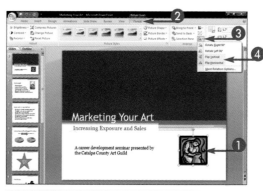

FLIP OBJECTS

① Click the object to select it.

② Click the Format tab.

③ Click the Rotate button.

In some cases, as when you have selected a SmartArt Graphic, you have to click an Align button on the Format tab to find the Rotate choice.

④ Click Flip Vertical or Flip Horizontal.

PowerPoint flips the object 180 degrees in the selected direction.

ROTATE OBJECTS

① Click the object to rotate.

Handles appear around it, including a green rotation handle off the top.

② Drag the rotation handle to the left or right.

The object tilts as you drag. When you release the mouse, the object stays at the new angle.

Add WordArt

You can quickly apply interesting text effects by inserting a WordArt object. WordArt takes a word or phrase and converts it into a graphic object that applies artistic styles, colors, and shapes to the text. WordArt is therefore useful for titles, logos, and any time you want text to really stand out from its surroundings.

You can also bend WordArt text and apply interesting color styles. After you add a WordArt object, you can move, resize, or format it using earlier techniques in this chapter.

Add WordArt

① With the slide on which you want to insert WordArt displayed in Normal view, click the Insert tab.

② Click WordArt.

The WordArt gallery appears.

③ Click a WordArt style.

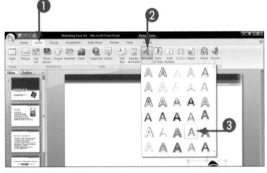

The WordArt object appears on the slide.

④ Type a word or phrase.

As you type, the WordArt text automatically sizes itself.

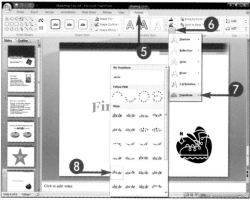

⑤ Click the Format tab.

⑥ Click the Text Effects button.

⑦ Point to Transform.

⑧ Click the desired shape in the gallery that appears.

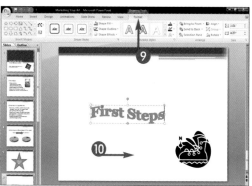

PowerPoint applies the transformed shape to the WordArt object.

⑨ Use other tools on the Format tab to change the WordArt object's appearance as desired.

⑩ Click outside the object to finish it.

TIP

Change It!

What happens if you create a WordArt object and then realize that it contains a typo? To fix the problem, click the WordArt object just like any text box or placeholder. The insertion point appears within the WordArt object so that you can make the necessary changes.

PowerPoint 2007 offers a number of tools for formatting and editing pictures, including tools that enable you to perform relatively sophisticated tasks such as recoloring the image and changing its brightness and contrast. PowerPoint also offers a number of useful effects beyond the shadow and 3-D effects you saw earlier in this chapter.

When you insert a digital image file, whether it is your own or a piece of clip art, you can edit it using the contextual Picture Tools that appear on the Format tab. You can change the brightness of the picture, modify the picture contrast, and *recolor* the picture, which applies a coloring effect to the picture, such as sepia, washout, or a color accent. You can also add a border to the picture and crop out part of the picture.

DISPLAY THE PICTURE TOOLS

① Insert and/or select a picture on a slide.

② Click the Format tab.

CHANGE IMAGE TONE, BORDER, OR COLORING

① Click Brightness, Contrast, Recolor, or Picture Border.

② Click the desired choice in the menu that appears.

● The change appears on the image.

CROP THE PICTURE

1. Click the Crop button.

● Black corner and side markers appear around the picture, and the mouse pointer changes to a cropping tool.

2. Drag a marker inward to remove an edge portion of the picture.

   When you release the mouse button, the image appears cropped.

3. Click the Crop button again to turn off the tool.

ADD A PICTURE STYLE

1. Click the More button in the Picture Styles group.

   The gallery of picture styles appears.

2. Click the desired style.

● PowerPoint applies the new style to the picture.

TIP

More Options!
Image files can get very large. When you insert them into your presentation, your PowerPoint file itself can become quite large. This may slow down PowerPoint's performance when you give a presentation. To make your file smaller, compress the pictures to remove redundant or unnecessary data without affecting image quality. On the Format tab, click the Compress Pictures button and then click OK.

You can group two or more objects together and work with them as a unit. This is useful if you often combine two or more graphic objects to create a more complex image. For example, you may use ovals and lines to create a drawing of a car. Once you have done that, you may need to work with all those objects at once. For example, you might want to change the colors of all the objects.

The easiest way to work with multiple objects together is to create a *group* consisting of all the objects. PowerPoint treats a group as a single object, so you can format, resize, and rotate the group the same way that you perform these actions on a single object.

GROUP OBJECTS

1. Select the objects to group.

2. Click the Format tab.

Note: *If you see two Format tabs, click either one.*

3. Click the Group button.

4. Click Group.

   A single selection box appears around the grouped object.

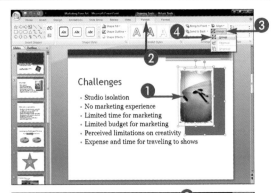

UNGROUP OBJECTS

1. Select the grouped object.

2. Click the Format tab.

Note: *If you see two Format tabs, click either one.*

3. Click the Group button.

4. Click Ungroup.

   The objects become separated once again.

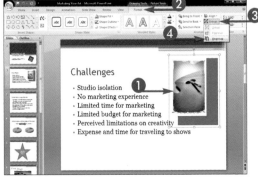

You can create special effects and ensure that your graphics are displayed properly by changing the stacking order of the objects.

When you have two graphic objects that overlap, the most recently created object covers part of the earlier object. The newer object is stacked in front of the older one. You can change the stacking

order either by sending an object towards the back of the stack or by bringing an object towards the front of the stack. For example, if you want to create a framed effect for a picture, the shape that you use as a frame must be behind the picture. Controlling stacking is called *arranging* or *ordering* the objects.

1. Select the object to arrange.

2. Click the Format tab.

3. Click Bring to Front.

   The object moves to the top of the stack.

4. Click the top object.

5. Click Send to Back.

   The object moves to the bottom of the stack.

   To stack the object forward one layer, click the Bring to Front button, and then click Bring Forward; to send the object back one layer, click the Send to Back button, and then click Send Backward.

PowerPoint offers two features — the grid and guidelines — that help you position objects and placeholders more precisely.

One of the little things that differentiates a solid presentation design from an amateur one is the proper alignment of objects on each slide. For example, if you have two or three clip art images running along the bottom of a slide, this arrangement looks best when the bottom edges of each

image are aligned. To help out, you can use the grid, which appears like graph paper lines on your slide. PowerPoint also offers the drawing guides, which are dashed lines — one vertical and one horizontal — that display over the slide area. When you click and drag an object near one of these guidelines, PowerPoint snaps the object to the line.

1. Click an object such as a shape or picture.
2. Click the Format tab.
3. Click the Align button.
4. Click Grid Settings.

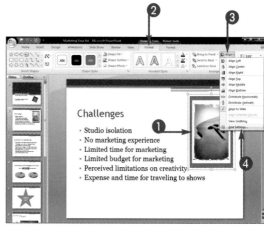

The Grid and Guides dialog box appears.

5. Click the Display grid on screen check box to check it.
6. Click the Display drawing guides on screen check box to check it.
7. Click OK.

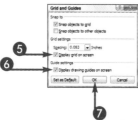

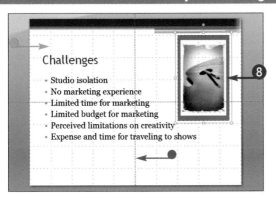

● The grid appears as dotted lines.

● The dashed guidelines intersect in the center of the slide.

⑧ Select and drag an object to line it up with the grid or guide.

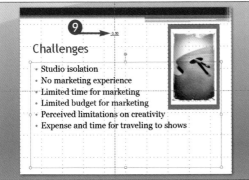

⑨ Drag a guideline.

A value representing the new position of the guide appears as you drag.

Redisplay the Grid and Guides dialog box and clear the boxes you checked in steps 4 and 5 to hide the grid and guidelines.

More Options!
PowerPoint also offers the Snap To feature that enables you to get objects to line up automatically along grid lines. Open the Grid and Guides dialog box. Click the Snap Objects to Grid option to select it, if needed, and then click OK. Now when you move an object around the slide, if it is close to a grid line, it automatically snaps to align with the grid.

You can accurately move objects in very small increments by nudging the objects. PowerPoint's grid and drawing guides (discussed in the previous section) are great for aligning objects. However, there are times when you want to arrange objects in some way other than aligning them along their edges. You can do this most quickly by clicking and dragging the objects with your mouse, but that's not the most accurate method. If you need precise positioning of an object, the Nudge drawing feature enables you to move a selected object by a small increment to the right, left, up, or down on the slide.

① Select the object to nudge.

② Press Down arrow, Left arrow, Right arrow, or Up arrow as many times as needed to nudge the object in the desired direction.

Press and hold Ctrl along with an arrow key to nudge the object by a smaller increment.

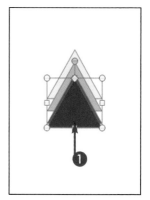

● The object moves in the specified direction.

③ Click outside the object to deselect it.

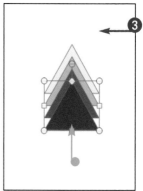

You can make your slides look neat and polished by aligning objects relative to each other. Unfortunately, aligning edges is not always easy, particularly if you use your mouse to do it. One way to work around this problem is to take advantage of PowerPoint's Align commands, which enable you to align a selection of objects on their edges (left, right, top, and bottom), on the horizontal center of their frames, or on the vertical middle of their frames.

PowerPoint also enables you to *distribute* objects so that they are evenly spaced relative to each other. You can distribute objects horizontally or vertically.

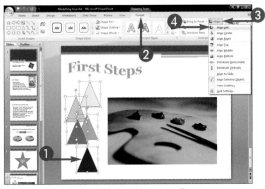

ALIGN OBJECTS

1. Select the objects to align.

2. Click the Format tab.

3. Click Align.

4. Click the desired alignment command.

   The objects align.

DISTRIBUTE OBJECTS

1. Select the objects to distribute.

2. Click the Format tab.

3. Click Align.

4. Click Distribute Horizontally or Distribute Vertically.

   The objects are distributed accordingly.

Chapter 1

Organizing Slides

After you have created a number of slides, you need to check to ensure that the overall flow of your presentation makes sense. The best place to organize your slides is in Slide Sorter view. This view displays a thumbnail (little pictures) of each slide. You can use the thumbnails to organize slides with ease.

In this chapter, you learn how to use Slide Sorter to move a slide from one part of a presentation to another; you learn how to

make a copy of an existing slide; you learn how to delete slides that you no longer require; you learn how to make a duplicate of an existing slide; you learn how to temporarily hide a slide from view; you learn how to zoom in on a slide to get a colder look at its contents; you learn how to use Slide Sorter view to quickly navigate to a particular slide; and you learn how to switch the Slide Sorter view between color and grayscale to make it easier to view the slides.

Quick Tips

You can ensure that your slides are presented in the correct order by moving slides into their proper position within the presentation.

A good presentation conveys a sequence of ideas that leads the viewer in a logical progression. When creating a presentation, you often have to reorganize slides to get that sequence just right.

You also may want to rearrange slides to create a variation of the original presentation that places the emphasis on different ideas. For example, in a presentation summarizing a company's previous fiscal year, you may want to move sales-related slides nearer to the beginning of the presentation when you present it to the Sales department; similarly, you may want to move marketing-related slides closer to the start for a Marketing department presentation.

① If using a view other than Slide Sorter view, click the Slide Sorter button.

The Slide Sorter view appears.

② Drag a slide thumbnail to the desired new location.

A line appears to indicate the new slide position.

When you release the mouse button, the slide appears in its new position.

Press and hold the Ctrl key as you drag to make a copy of the selected slide.

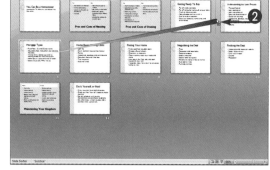

You can avoid repeating work by making a copy of an existing slide. This is particularly useful when you are dealing with complex slides that use a custom layout, incorporate lots of text and other objects, and use extensive custom formatting. Such a slide can take a great deal of time to create and customize to your liking. If you create presentations about similar subjects, you can save a great deal of time by copying a slide from an existing presentation and then pasting it into your current presentation. Even if you have to make small changes to the copy, it will still be much faster than re-creating the slide from scratch.

To copy a slide within the same presentation, you can save a few steps by duplicating the slide. See "Make a Duplicate Slide" later in this chapter.

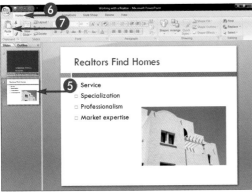

① With a PowerPoint presentation open in Slide Sorter view, select the slide(s) you want to copy.

Shift+click or Ctrl+click to select multiple thumbnails.

② Click the Home tab.

③ Click the Copy button.

④ Open another presentation.

If the other presentation is already open, click the View tab, click Switch Windows, and then click the presentation name.

⑤ In any view or pane, click the slide after which you want the copied slide to appear.

⑥ Click the Home tab, if needed.

⑦ Click the Paste button.

The copied slide(s) appear in the presentation, after the slide selected in step 5.

You can keep your presentations focused and uncluttered by removing unneeded slides.

As you build your presentation, you may find that a particular slide contains information that you no longer need, that is no longer relevant, or that is out of date. You may also find that you do not like the layout, contents, or formatting of a particular slide, and that fixing the slide would require a great deal of work. For all these situations, PowerPoint enables you to delete from the presentation any slide that you no longer require.

Note, too, that if you often create a presentation using a content template or a copy of another presentation file, then you typically may need to delete multiple slides that do not suit your purpose.

① **With a PowerPoint presentation open in Slide Sorter view, select the slide(s) you want to delete.**

You can use Ctrl+click to select more than one slide to delete.

② **Click the Home tab.**

③ **Click the Delete button.**

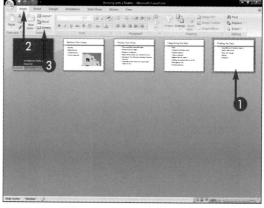

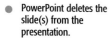

● **PowerPoint deletes the slide(s) from the presentation.**

PowerPoint does not prompt you to confirm the deletion. If you want to get the slide back, press Ctrl+Z or click Undo immediately.

If you have a slide in the current presentation that has similar content and formatting to what you want for a new slide, you can save yourself a great deal of time by inserting a duplicate of that slide and then adjusting the copy as needed.

It is quite common to have two or more slides with similar content. For example, you may want to present slides containing goals for the Eastern and Western Divisions,

some of which will be common to both. Rather than retyping the common text in the second slide, it is faster to create a duplicate of the first slide and then adjust the copy accordingly.

Similarly, if a slide at the beginning of the presentation lists the key topics, you can duplicate that slide and use it again at the end to wrap up or summarize.

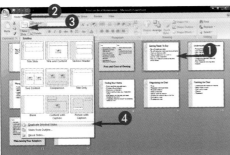

① **Working in Slide Sorter view, click the slide you want to duplicate.**

② **Click the Home tab.**

③ **Click the New Slide button.**

④ **Click Duplicate Selected Slides.**

● **A copy of the slide is pasted to the right of the currently selected slide.**

You can create custom presentations tailored to different groups by hiding those slides that each group does not need to see.

Hiding a slide prevents it from displaying during an onscreen slide show. By hiding slides, you can create mini-presentations from a master presentation without deleting any slides. You can hide slides, give the presentation, and then unhide

them. For example, a budget presentation may include sensitive financial data. It is okay to present that data to company executives, but you would not want to present that data to company outsiders such as analysts and investors. In that case, you can hide the sensitive slides.

You also may want to hide a few slides temporarily to see how your presentation flows without them.

① **Working in Slide Sorter view, select the slide(s) you want to hide.**

Ctrl+click to select more than one slide.

② **Click the Slide Show tab.**

③ **Click Hide Slide.**

You also can right-click the selected thumbnail(s), and then click Hide Slide in the submenu.

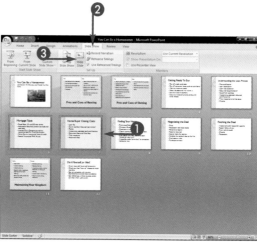

● **A gray box and diagonal line appear on the slide number, indicating it will not display when you show the slide show.**

④ **To redisplay hidden slide(s), repeat steps 1 to 3.**

You can make it easier to view and find slides in Slide Sorter view by zooming in on or out of the view.

In Slide Sorter view, there is a trade-off between seeing more slide thumbnails and seeing the detail on each slide. Viewing more slide thumbnails helps you see the big picture of your presentation, enables you to quickly find the slide you want, and makes it easier to rearrange slides.

However, the more slide thumbnails you see, the smaller each slide appears, which makes it harder to recognize the slide you want to work with.

You can work between viewing more slide thumbnails and viewing slide detail by changing the Zoom level. To see more slide thumbnails, you select a smaller zoom percentage; to see more slide detail, you select a larger zoom percentage.

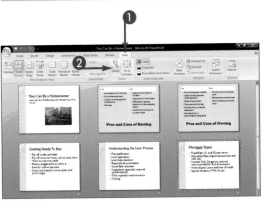

① Working in Slide Sorter view, click the View tab.

② Click Zoom.

You also can drag the Zoom slider or click one of the buttons at the ends of the slider to zoom. The Zoom slider appears in the lower-right corner of the PowerPoint window.

The Zoom dialog box appears.

③ Click the option button for the desired zoom level.

● You can also click the spinner arrows or type a percentage here.

④ Click OK.

PowerPoint displays the slides at the specified zoom level.

You can use Slide Sorter view to quickly open a slide in Normal view.

Slide Sorter view is useful for seeing the overall organization of your presentation and for rearranging the slides. However, you cannot work on a slide in Slide Sorter view, and if the Zoom percentage is too small, you may not be able to see much detail on a slide. When you are working in

Slide Sorter view, it is sometimes useful to switch to Normal view where you can work with a slide to view the slide in detail.

Although you can select a slide and then click the Normal view icon, these steps show a faster way to display an individual slide.

---

1 Working in Slide Sorter view, double-click the slide you want to display in Normal view.

The slide appears in the Normal view.

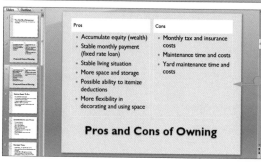

In a presentation with a lot of color in the background, it can be easier to see thumbnail content in Slide Sorter view in grayscale or black and white.

Slide Sorter view displays a thumbnail version of a presentation's slides. These thumbnails are miniature versions of the actual slides and, by default, PowerPoint also includes each slide's color formatting

in the thumbnail. This is usually what you want because seeing each slide's coloring gives you an accurate picture of the slide's look.

However, you may find that the colors are distracting, particularly if you use many vivid colors. In that case, you can switch to grayscale, which presents slides in black, white, and shades of gray.

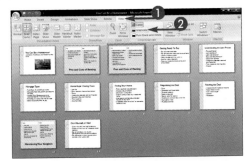

① Working in Slide Sorter view, click the View tab.

You also can view slides in grayscale or black and white in Normal view.

② Click Grayscale or click Pure Black and White.

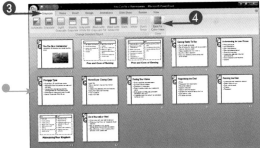

● The presentation appears in grayscale or black and white depending on your choice.

Depending on the button you clicked, a Grayscale or a Black and White tab appears, offering additional viewing options and a Back to Color View button.

③ After working, click the Grayscale or Black and White tab to return to it.

④ Click Back to Color View.

The presentation reappears in color.

Adding Action to Slides

In PowerPoint, *animation* refers to applying motion to text or objects on slides. Action buttons enable interaction with an onscreen slide show.

Adding animation to slide objects causes them to appear at different times, with special motion. You might animate a set of bullet points, for example, to slide in one at a time from the top of the screen. You could animate a clip art object to move across your screen from left to right, or use an animation to cause your company logo to spin around on the slide.

Animations help you add emphasis to text or an object on a slide. If audience attention drifts after a long explanation or technical discussion, animations can help audience members refocus. You should avoid

overusing animations, which makes your presentation seem busy and can overshadow the presentation's content. Use animations sparingly, and they will serve as attention grabbers that help presentation pace.

Transitions offer a way to add variety to your presentation. With transitions, you can modify how slides are displayed when they first appear. You also can set up PowerPoint to time a transition to occur at various speeds.

A transition effect occurs when you advance a slide show from one slide to another. Movies use transitions—for example, when you see the screen dissolve from one image to another, or you see an image seem to wipe across the screen to reveal another scene.

Quick Tips

Apply an Animation

You can use the Animations tab on the Ribbon to apply an animation to any selected slide object. PowerPoint 2007 comes with a number of predefined animations for different types of objects. In each case, you have the choice of three animation types: Fade, Wipe, and Fly In.

How you apply these effects depends on the object. For example, with a slide title, picture, clip art, or table, the animation effect applies to the entire object; with a bulleted list, you can apply the animation effect to the entire list or by first-level paragraphs; for a chart, you can apply the animation effect to individual chart elements, such as a series or category; and for SmartArt, you can apply the animation effect to individual SmartArt graphic elements, such as a level or a branch.

① Select the object to animate.

You can select any kind of object: a placeholder, text box, picture, or WordArt.

You can Shift+click to select multiple objects and apply the animation to all at once.

② Click the Animations tab.

③ Click the Animate drop-down list.

④ Click the desired animation to apply.

PowerPoint applies the animation to the object.

Note: If Live Preview is active, PowerPoint previews any animation that you point to in the Animate drop-down list, enabling you to see how the effect looks before clicking to select it.

⑤ Click elsewhere on the slide to deselect the object.

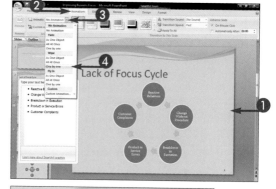

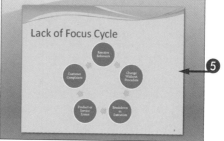

You can make sure that an animation does what you want by previewing the effect in Normal view.

A simple animation effect is straightforward and should offer no surprises. As your animations become more complex, however, you cannot always be certain that you are achieving the effect you want. To ensure that you know what each animation effect does, and to help you modify your

animations when necessary, you should preview the effect. You can play the animation in Normal view without having to start the slide show, or you can run the slide show using a button on the Animations tab of the Ribbon. Previewing the regular or custom animations applied to a slide enables you to verify that the animations work as expected and are appropriate for the slide's content.

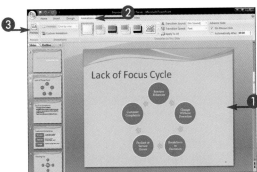

① Display the slide with the animation(s) to preview in Normal view.

② Click the Animations tab.

③ Click the Preview button.

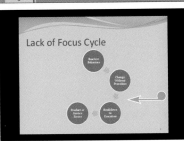

● The animation previews in the Slide pane.

You also can preview the animations by running the entire slide show. Click the Slide Show button or press F5 to run the slide show. After it plays, press Esc at the final black screen to return to working in PowerPoint.

Add a Custom Animation

You can get complete control over your animation effects by applying a custom animation to any selected object on a slide.

The predefined animation effects look great and save you tons of time, but they have one very large drawback: You cannot customize them directly. For example, you cannot change properties such as the speed and direction of the animation. Also, some of the schemes do not work the way you might want. For example,

one highly requested visual effect is to display bullet points one at a time. A predefined animation effect named By first level paragraphs is available, but it is not useful because you cannot control when each bullet appears.

To solve all these problems and to create unique and visually appealing animations, you need to design them yourself using PowerPoint's Custom Animation pane.

① With the object to animate selected and the Animations tab displayed, click the Custom Animation button.

The Custom Animation task pane appears.

② Click Add Effect.

③ Click a category.

④ Click an effect.

PowerPoint applies the effect and previews it.

The animation appears in the Custom Animation task pane. The numbers beside the listed animations indicate the order in which the animations will play.

⑤ Click an animation to select it in the Custom Animation task pane.

⑥ Click here and select an option for starting the animation when running the slide show.

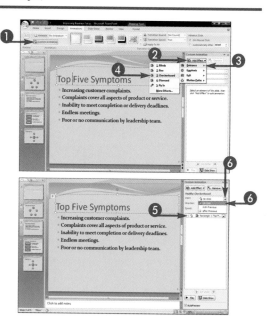

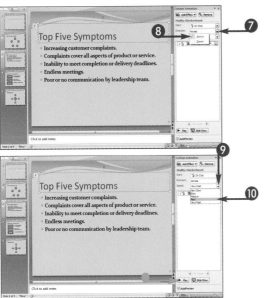

⑦ Click the Direction list's menu.

⑧ Click a direction or path option.

PowerPoint applies the setting.

⑨ Click the Speed list's menu.

⑩ Click the speed to apply to the transition.

● You can click Play to preview your settings.

The animation plays.

More Options!
You can control the timing and repetition of animations. Click the down-arrow button to the right of the animation in the Custom Animation task pane list and then click Timing. In the dialog box that appears, click the Timing tab and type a number (in seconds) in the Delay field. You can also click in the Repeat field and select the number of times you want the animation to repeat. When you click OK to close the dialog box, PowerPoint applies the delay timing.

Reorder Animations

If you have applied multiple animations to a slide, you can ensure the proper effect by arranging the animations in the order in which you want them to appear.

PowerPoint enables you to add multiple animation effects to a slide. For example, you might set up a slide so that the bullet points fly in one at a time each time you click the mouse. This is useful if you do

not want your audience to see all the bullets in advance. However, for such an effect to be successful, you need to ensure that the bullet animations occur in the order that you want the bullets to appear. If they do not, you can change the order in which the animated objects play when the slide appears during the slide show.

① With the Custom Animation task pane displayed and several animations applied, click the animation to reorder.

Note: See the section "Add a Custom Animation" to learn how to display the Custom Animation task pane.

② Click either the Move Up or the Move Down button to reposition the animation.

● The item moves up or down in the list accordingly.

If no animations appear below the item, Move Down is unavailable. If no animations appear above the item, then Move Up is unavailable.

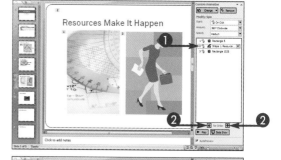

If you have a slide that contains an animation effect you no longer need, you can remove that effect from the slide.

You should avoid the temptation to use many different animations in a single slide. Just as slide text looks awful if you use too many fonts or colors, your presentations will look amateurish if you use too many animated effects. If you run the slide show and decide that you have

overdone the animations, you scan remove some of them. You can remove both standard and custom animations from slide objects. If you apply a custom animation and decide you want to use another animation, you have to remove the first one, or you end up with two animations on that single object. Remove the animation from the Animations tab or the Custom Animation task pane.

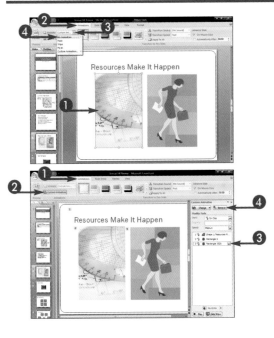

REMOVE FROM THE ANIMATIONS TAB

1. In Normal view, select the object(s) from which you want to remove an animation.

2. Click the Animations tab.

3. Click the Animate drop-down list.

4. Click No Animation.

   PowerPoint removes the animation.

REMOVE FROM THE TASK PANE

1. In Normal view, click the Animations tab.

2. Click the Custom Animation button.

   The Custom Animation task pane appears.

3. Click an animation in the list.

4. Click Remove.

   PowerPoint removes the animation effect from the object.

Insert an Action Button

You can use action buttons to easily configure basic navigation shapes and other dynamic objects for your presentation.

Not all presentations proceed from one slide to the next. For example, someone in the audience may ask you to return to the previous slide because he or she missed something or has a question. Similarly, you may need to return to a previously viewed slide for further discussion or clarification.

To make this kind of navigation easy, you can add *action buttons*, which are special shape objects with icons that represent their functions. For example, there are action buttons for Previous, Next, Beginning, and End. You can also link to a Web page or open a document.

INSERT A BUTTON

1. With the slide on which you want to insert the action button displayed in Normal view, click the Insert tab.

2. Click the Shapes button.

3. Click a button style.

   The mouse pointer turns into a crosshair (+).

4. Drag diagonally on the slide to create the action button.

ESTABLISH A HYPERLINK

An action button and the Action Settings dialog box appear.

5. If the Hyperlink to option button is not selected, click it.

6. Click here and select the slide you want to appear when the action button is clicked.

   Depending on your choice, the last slide appears or a dialog box appears for you to type a URL.

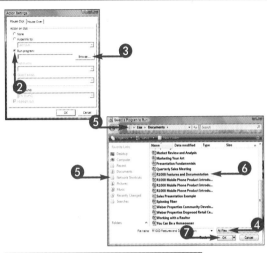

OPEN A DOCUMENT

1. Perform steps **1** to **4** on the previous page.

   The Action Settings dialog box appears.

2. Click Run Program.

3. Click Browse.

   The Select a Program to Run dialog box appears.

4. Click here and click All Files.

5. Navigate to the folder holding the file to open.

6. Click the file to open with the action button.

7. Click OK.

   The Action Settings dialog box reappears.

8. Click OK in the Action Settings dialog box.

   ● The action button is finalized on the slide.

Try This!

If you want to include a hyperlink, but you do not want to clutter the slide with an action button icon, you can create a text hyperlink on your slide. Using this feature, you can, for example, make your slide title function as a hyperlink so that clicking it during a slide show follows the link. See the section "Insert a Hyperlink" for more about this.

Add a Transition

You can add visual interest and a professional look to your presentations by including transitions from one slide to another.

A *slide transition* is a special effect that displays the next slide in the presentation. For example, in a *fade* transition, the next slide gradually materializes, whereas in a *blinds* transition the next slide appears with an effect similar to opening Venetian blinds. PowerPoint has nearly 60 different slide transitions, and for each one, you can control the transition speed, the sound effect that goes along with the transition, and the trigger for the transition (a mouse click or a time interval). Applying a transition from the Random category tells PowerPoint to apply a different transition for each slide in the presentation.

---

① With the slide to which you want to apply a transition selected in Normal view, click the Animations tab.

② Click the More button beside the transitions gallery in the Transitions To This Slide group.

The gallery of available transitions appears.

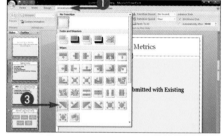

③ Click a transition in the gallery, scrolling down first if needed.

● PowerPoint applies the transition to the slide or selected slides, and the effect previews.

● A star appears beside the slide's thumbnail to indicate the transition has been applied.

● To apply the transition to all slides, click Apply to All.

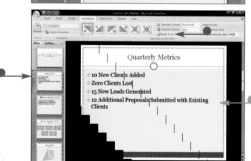

You can avoid distracting your audience by removing any transitions that are unnecessary or unsuitable.

A slide transition is only as useful as it is unremarkable. If everybody leaves your presentation thinking "Nice transitions!", then you have a problem because they should be thinking about your message.

Simple transitions such as fades, wipes, and dissolves add interest but do not get in the way. On the other hand, if you have objects flying in from all corners of the screen, your content will seem like a letdown. If you have added any transitions that might get in the way of your message, PowerPoint enables you to remove those transitions from your presentation.

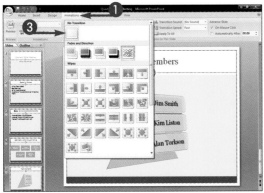

① With the slide to which you want to remove a transition selected in Normal view, click the Animations tab.

② Click the More button beside the transitions gallery in the Transitions To This Slide group.

The gallery of available transitions appears.

③ Click the transition icon under No Transition.

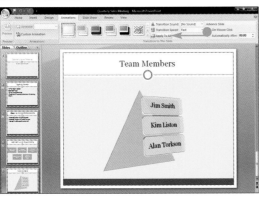

PowerPoint removes any existing transition.

● To remove transitions from all slides in the presentation, you can click Apply to All.

Advance a Slide After a Set Time Interval

You can set up an automatic slide show by configuring each slide to advance to the next slide after a specified interval.

What do you do if you want to show a presentation at a trade show, fair, or other public event, but you cannot have a person presenting the slide show? Similarly, what do you do if you want

to send a presentation to a customer or prospect and you cannot be there to go through the slide show yourself?

For these and similar situations, you can configure each slide to advance automatically after a certain number of seconds or minutes has elapsed.

① With the slide for which you want to set an advance timing selected in Normal view, click the Animations tab.

② Click Automatically After.

③ Click the spinner arrows to set the time interval.

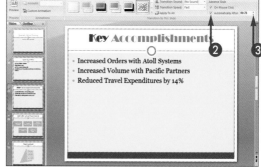

④ Click the Slide Sorter buttons.

Slide Sorter view appears.

● A notation of the time interval set appears under the slide.

If you leave the On Mouse Click check box checked, you can advance the slide more quickly by clicking your mouse.

You can further customize a transition by setting a transition speed. The transition speed controls the rate at which the transition effect plays. For transitions such as wipes, you might prefer a faster speed that keeps the slide show moving. For fade and dissolve transitions, you might prefer a slow transition speed so that the audience gets the full effect.

Note, however, that many people prefer to use the Fast settings for all transitions. This ensures that the transition from one slide to another never takes more than a few seconds. Along similar lines, you should avoid running multiple object animations at the same time because it can take an awfully long time for the effect to finish, and audiences never like having their time wasted on such things.

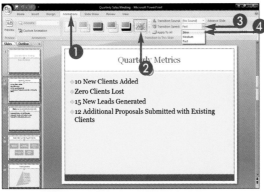

① With the slide to which you want to add a transition speed selected in Normal view, click the Animations tab.

② Apply the desired transition to the slide.

Note: See the section "Add a Transition" to apply a transition.

③ Click the Transition Speed drop-down list.

④ Click the desired speed.

● PowerPoint previews the specified transition using the speed setting that you selected.

Insert Movie and Sound Clips

To make your slide show livelier, you can insert a movie or sound clip on a slide and then play it during the show. You can insert a movie or sound file from the Insert tab on the Ribbon.

You can use the Media Clip icon in any content placeholder to insert movie and sound clips, as explained in Chapter 2. If

you insert a media file such as a video, music clip, or sound file into a slide, PowerPoint gives you two choices for playing the media: Automatically or When Clicked. Select Automatically to have PowerPoint play the media as soon as you navigate to the slide; select When Clicked to have PowerPoint play the media only when you click it.

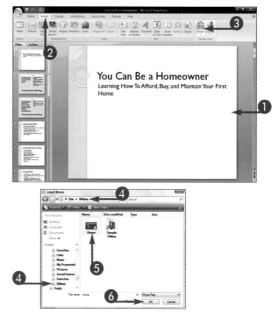

① In Normal view, display the slide on which you want to insert a clip.

② Click the Insert tab.

③ Click the top portion of either the Movie or Sound button in the Media Clips group.

The Insert Movie or Insert Sound dialog box appears.

If you click the bottom of either button, a menu of different options, such as inserting a clip from Clip Organizer, appears.

④ If needed, navigate to the folder holding the video or sound to insert.

⑤ Click the clip you want to insert.

⑥ Click OK.

PowerPoint asks how you want the movie or sound to start during the show.

⑦ Click either Automatically or When Clicked.

⑧ Resize an inserted movie clip as needed. Also position the movie clip or the icon for the sound clip as desired.

Note: See Chapter 5 to learn how to work with media content you add to a slide.

If you did not specify that the movie or sound should play automatically during the slide show, click the movie frame or sound icon on the slide to start the playback.

Change It!

If you want to change the way a movie or sound plays back during the slide show, switch to Normal view, and then click the movie frame or the sound icon. Then click the Movie Tools or Sound Tools contextual tab on the Ribbon to find the settings for controlling how the movie or sound plays.

Insert a Hyperlink

You can add an element of dynamism to your slides by inserting hyperlinks that take you immediately to another slide, document, or Web page.

When running a presentation, you may find it advantageous to temporarily exit the presentation by displaying a Web site or opening another document. You may also need to jump to a specific slide in the

same presentation. You can do all of this by inserting a *hyperlink*. A hyperlink is a word or phrase in a text box, SmartArt graphic, picture, or clip art image that acts just like a link in a Web page or document. That is, when you click the link, the linked Web page or document appears.

---

① Select a title or text placeholder on a slide.

② Click the Insert tab.

③ Click the Hyperlink button.

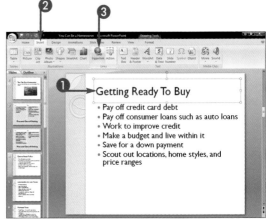

The Insert Hyperlink dialog box appears.

④ Click the kind of link to insert.

In this example, Place in This Document is selected.

Depending on what you select in step 4, different options appear.

⑤ Locate or type the slide, document, Web page, or e-mail address in the appropriate fields.

⑥ Click OK.

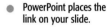

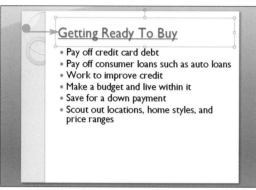

Getting Ready To Buy

- Pay off credit card debt
- Pay off consumer loans such as auto loans
- Work to improve credit
- Make a budget and live within it
- Save for a down payment
- Scout out locations, home styles, and price ranges

● PowerPoint places the link on your slide.

When you run the slide show, you can click the text to follow the link.

More Options!

What do you do if you do not want to enter a lot of text for the link itself, but would like to let the person running the presentation know exactly what it leads to? Create a ScreenTip. In the Insert Hyperlink dialog box, click the ScreenTip button and enter as much text as you like in the dialog box that appears. Click OK and finish creating the link from there. Now when the person running the show holds the mouse over the link, the tip appears in a little box.

Set Up a Slide Show

After you add your slide content, tweak your slide design, and add graphics, animations, and transitions, you are almost done. In this chapter, you take the final steps to set up your presentation options.

It is always a good idea to solicit feedback about a presentation before delivering it, and you will learn how to send a presentation via e-mail for another person to review it. You will also learn how to add comments to a presentation and how to review and remove comments.

A big part of getting your slide show set up is deciding which options you need. These

options include whether the show should repeat continuously, whether you want to use narration and animations, the pen color for annotations, which slides to include in the show, and which screen resolution to use. You learn about these and other options in this chapter.

One of the keys to a good presentation is to rehearse the entire slide show before presenting. This not only helps you learn your material, but PowerPoint also enables you to time the delivery of each slide and to save those timings. You can also record narration to play along with some or all of the slide show.

Quick Tips

Send a Presentation for Review

You can improve your overall presentation by soliciting feedback from another person via e-mail.

In all endeavors, an extra pair of eyes is an extremely useful way to get a fresh perspective on your work. With a presentation, you may want or be required to seek feedback on your content before you give your presentation. A second opinion helps because another reader can spot errors you missed or suggest improvements. PowerPoint enables you to solicit such feedback by giving you the capability to e-mail your presentation to another person.

After you e-mail a file for review, the recipient adds comments into the file. The person e-mails the file back, and you can review and implement ideas as needed.

SEND A FILE

Note: These steps assume that your e-mail program is properly configured to work with other applications.

1. Click Office.

2. Point to Send.

3. Click E-mail.

An e-mail message window appears.

4. Type the recipient's e-mail address.

5. Click here to edit or type additional text for the message.

6. Click Send.

PowerPoint and your e-mail program send the message with the presentation attached.

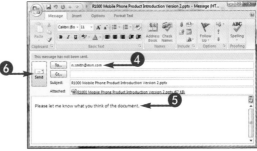

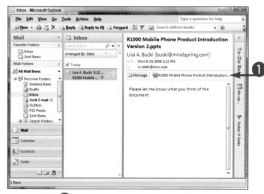

OPEN A REVIEWED FILE

① When you receive a file back from a reviewer, double-click the file to open it.

Note: If Windows asks whether you want to save or open the presentation, you can click Open to open it directly or click Save to save it to your hard disk. Chapter 2 describes how to save and open files.

The presentation opens on screen.

② Review the comments in the presentation.

Note: See the section "Review and Delete Comments" to learn more.

Important!

You may find that your recipient cannot open your PowerPoint 2007 file. In that case, PowerPoint 2007 enables you to save files in a format compatible with older PowerPoint versions. To save in a compatible format before sending, click Office, point to the arrow at the right end of the Save As command, and then click PowerPoint 97-2003 Format. The Save As dialog box opens with the proper file type specified, so you can finish the save.

You can add feedback to a presentation by inserting comments that are tied to individual slides or slide objects.

If someone asks for your feedback on a presentation, you could write that feedback in a separate document or an e-mail message. However, if you have a suggestion or critique of a particular slide or slide object, the reader will understand that feedback more readily if it appears

near the object in question. To do that in PowerPoint, you insert a *comment*, a separate section of text that is associated with some part of the original presentation. PowerPoint identifies each comment with a sticky note icon, making it easy for the author to find and consider each comment. After you add your comments, save the file and e-mail it or otherwise send it to the author.

① Working in Normal view, display the slide on which you want to add a comment.

② Click the Review tab.

③ Click the New Comment button.

If you want the comment to be next to a particular object on the slide, select that object after step 2.

The comment marker and box appear.

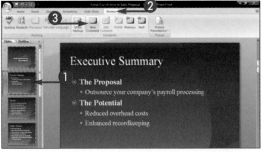

④ Type the comment text.

⑤ Click outside the comment box.

The comment box closes, leaving only the comment marker visible onscreen.

⑥ Select other slides as needed and repeat steps **3** to **5** to add more comments.

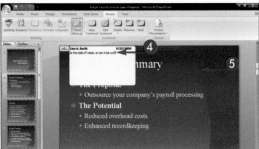

When you receive a presentation with added comments, you can review those comments and then delete them from the presentation.

After you send a presentation for review, the recipient runs through the presentation and uses the technique from the previous section to add comments. When that is done, the reviewer sends the presentation back to you. Your job now is to go through each of those comments and incorporate any suggestions that you think are worthwhile. When you have completed that, you probably do not want to leave the comments in the presentation, so you should delete them.

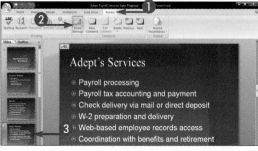

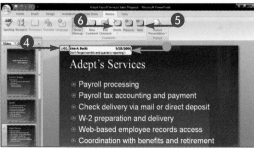

① Working in Normal view, click the Review tab.

② If the Show Markup button is not highlighted (active), click it.

Comment note markers appear.

③ Display a slide with a comment marker.

④ Click the comment marker.

● The comment box opens, so you can review the comment text.

⑤ Click the Previous and Next buttons to move between comments.

⑥ Click the Delete button to delete the current comment.

Comments do print by default when you print slides. Delete unneeded comments before printing or clear the Print Comments and Ink Markup check box in the Print dialog box.

Select a Show Type and Show Options

You can configure your slide show to suit the type of show you want to run. PowerPoint maintains a number of slide show options, so before you run your show for the first time, you should check the settings for the type of show, and some of the options for running the show. These options include whether the show should repeat continuously, whether you want to use narration and animations, and the pen color for annotations made onscreen during the show.

For example, you may have to run your slide show at a fair or trade show where there will not be a person to present the show. In this case, you can configure the slide show to use kiosk mode, using timer settings to advance the slides, and to loop continuously.

① With the presentation to set up open, click the Slide Show tab.

② Click the Set Up Slide Show button.

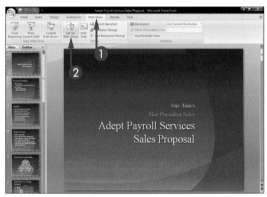

The Set Up Show dialog box appears.

③ Click an option button to select whether you want to have a speaker run the show, a viewer browse the show on a computer, or a viewer view the show at a kiosk.

● If you choose to let individuals browse the show, you can click the Show scrollbar check box to check it.

④ Click either the Manually (user clicks button to advance slides) or Using timings, if present (slides advance automatically) option button.

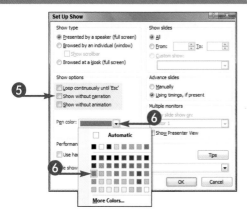

⑤ Select whether you want to loop through the show continuously, show it without narration, or show it without animation. You can check one or more of these options.

⑥ Click here and select a pen color from the palette.

This item is not available if you select any show type other than Presented by a Speaker.

⑦ Click OK.

Your show is set up.

Make sure that you save the presentation file to preserve slide show settings.

Caution!
Animations are fun, but on slower computer systems or those lacking adequate display memory, they may run slowly and delay your show. If you are using an older computer to present your show, preview it to be sure that animations run smoothly. If they do not, activate the Show without narration setting to avoid any problems.

Specify Slides to Include

Sometimes you create a larger presentation, but decide that for a particular audience you want to show only some of the slides. To limit the slides displayed, you can save a custom slide show or you can specify a range of slides to play back in the Set Up Show dialog box.

Having two or more versions of a presentation is common. For example,

you might have a short version and a long version of a presentation; you might want to omit certain slides depending on whether you are presenting to managers, salespeople, or engineers; or you might have "internal" and "external" versions; that is, you might have one version for people who work at your company and a different version for people from outside the company.

CREATE A CUSTOM SHOW

1. Click the Slide Show tab.

2. Click the Custom Slide Show button.

3. Click Custom Shows.

   The Custom Shows dialog box appears.

4. Click New.

   The Define Custom Show dialog box appears.

5. Type a name in the Slide show name text box.

6. Click a slide and click Add.

   Repeat step **6** to add all the slides you want to show.

7. Click OK.

8. Click Close in the Custom Shows dialog box to save the show.

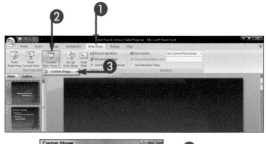

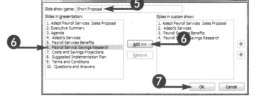

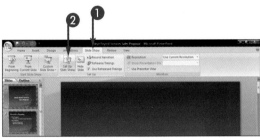

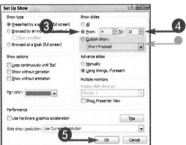

SPECIFY WHICH SLIDES TO SHOW

1. Click the Slide Show tab.

2. Click the Set Up Slide Show button.

   The Set Up Show dialog box appears.

3. Click From.

● If you saved a custom show, you can click the Custom show option button and then choose a show from the drop-down list to play back only its slides.

4. Enter the first and last slides to display in the From and To text boxes.

5. Click OK.

   PowerPoint saves the show settings. Only the specified slides will appear when you run the slide show.

Did You Know?

PowerPoint offers a quick way to display your custom show. Open the presentation in which you created the custom show. Click the Slide Show tab, and then click the Custom Slide Show button. The menu that appears includes the names of all custom shows you have saved in the file. Click the name of the custom slide show to play.

You can control the quality of slide show playback to accommodate different display devices, speed up playback, or ensure good presentation fidelity. For example, if you are preparing the slide show to play on a kiosk that can display only at 800×600, you should choose that resolution. If you want the fastest playback, choose the 640×480 resolution. Note, however, that this lower resolution may result in poorer presentation appearance. You should run through your presentation to see whether the lower resolution causes problems with any slides. For the best looking presentation, use the highest resolution you can. Most modern computers can run at 1024×768 resolution, so that is a good choice for high-fidelity playback.

① Click the Slide Show tab.

② Click the Set Up Slide Show button.

The Set Up Show dialog box appears.

③ Click here and select a resolution from the list.

④ Click OK.

PowerPoint saves the resolution setting and uses it when you subsequently run the slide show.

You also can click the Slide Show tab, click the Resolution drop-down list, and then click the desired resolution.

You can rehearse the timing of your slide show so that you know exactly how long it takes to present each slide.

With PowerPoint's Rehearse Timings feature, you run through ("rehearse") your presentation, and PowerPoint keeps track of the amount of time you spend on each slide. This is useful if you have only so much time to present the slide show, because Rehearse Timings lets you know

if your presentation runs too long or too short. Also, you can examine the time spent on each slide. If you have consecutive slides where you spend a short amount of time on each, consider consolidating two or more of the slides into a single slide. Conversely, if you have a slide where you spend a great deal of time, consider splitting it into two or more slides.

① With the slide show to rehearse open, click the Slide Show tab.

② Click the Rehearse Timings button.

The Rehearsal toolbar appears.

③ Rehearse the slide materials, clicking the Next button to advance to the next slide when needed.

After the last slide, a message box informs you of the total delivery time and asks whether you want to save the timings.

④ Click Yes to save timings, or No to exit the rehearsal without saving timings.

The presentation reappears in Slide Sorter view, where you can see the timing applied to each slide below its thumbnail.

You can record a narration that talks the viewer through your key points. For most slide shows, part of the appeal of a good presentation is that it feels like we are being told a story. Some words or images appear on a screen, but a person presents the underlying narrative for those words and images.

However, times may occur when you require a recorded voice for some or all of a presentation. For example, you might have a slide that consists of a recorded greeting from the CEO or someone else at your company. Similarly, you might be setting up an automatic presentation and so require recorded narration for the entire show. PowerPoint can handle all of these situations by enabling you to record narration from one or more slides or for the entire presentation.

① Plug a microphone into your computer.

② Click the Slide Show tab.

③ Click the Record Narration button.

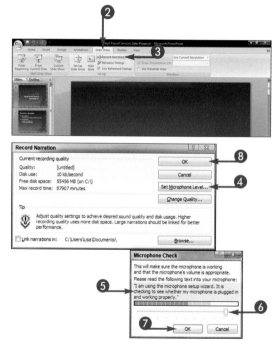

The Record Narration dialog box appears.

④ Click Set Microphone Level.

The Microphone Check dialog box opens.

⑤ Read the suggested text into your microphone.

PowerPoint checks that your microphone is working properly.

⑥ If the volume is wrong, drag the slider to change microphone volume.

⑦ Click OK.

⑧ Click OK in the Record Narration dialog box.

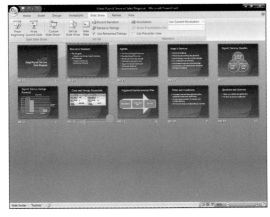

The presentation begins to run.

9 Speak your narration into your microphone, pressing Spacebar to advance to the next slide as needed.

10 When you finish the presentation, press Esc.

A message appears asking whether you want to save the timings.

11 Click Save.

The presentation appears in Slide Sorter view.

● The timing appears beneath each slide and reflects the length of its recorded narration.

After you record narration, remember to redisplay the Set Up Show dialog box to ensure that the Show Without Narration check box is unchecked.

More Options!
You may find that your narration sound quality is poor. To fix this, you can set the quality level for your narration. However, keep in mind that higher-quality recordings mean bigger presentation files. To adjust quality, click Change Quality in the Record Narration dialog box. Higher kHz settings result in higher-quality recordings.

Print Presentations

Most presentations exist only as electronic files. You create, work on, and save the presentation on your computer, and you may transfer the presentation file to a notebook computer for the presentation itself. The days of projecting overhead transparencies using acetate sheets may not be completely over, but thanks to PowerPoint their days are numbered.

That is not to say that you might never have to print out a PowerPoint presentation. In fact, there are a number of reasons why you might need to print all or part of a presentation. For example, if you are

making the presentation on the road, you may want a hard copy of your slides to review while you are away from your computer, say, on a plane. Perhaps most commonly, you might want to print handouts for your audience to follow during your live presentation. You might also need to print out your presentation if you need to fax it to someone who does not have a computer or Internet access. Finally, you might print just your presentation outline or notes to preserve a hard copy of the presentation text. This chapter shows you how to take advantage of PowerPoint's printing capabilities.

Quick Tips

You can see what your presentation looks like without printing it by using PowerPoint's Print Preview feature.

Before you consider printing a presentation, understand that doing so can be costly, particularly if your presentation is a long one. Not only do you use up paper, but slides with colorful or dark backgrounds can use up a lot of printer ink. This is made worse if, after printing, you find an error or decide that your presentation does not look the way you want it to. After you fix the problem, you must print the presentation yet again. Therefore, it is a good practice to see what your slides look like onscreen, before you use resources printing. To see what your printout will look like before printing, use the Print Preview feature.

① Click Office.

② Point to the arrow button at the right of the Print choice.

③ Click Print Preview.

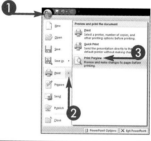

PowerPoint displays the slide show in the Print Preview view.

The Preview appears differently depending on whether the currently selected printer is a color or black and white printer. You can select another printer to use in the Print dialog box, which you see in later sections.

④ Click the Print What drop-down list to select another type of print output to view, if needed.

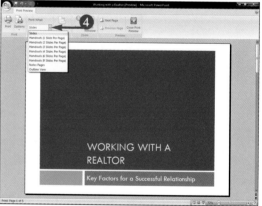

⑤ To navigate in the presentation, click the Next Page or Previous Page button.

⑥ To preview a grayscale printout (even if using a color printer), click here and select your options.

⑦ Finish your work in Print Preview by clicking a button.

● You can click Print to open the Print dialog box, verify print settings, and then print.

⑧ Click the Close Print Preview button.

PowerPoint closes the Print Preview.

More Options!
When you use Print Preview, the mouse pointer becomes a little magnifying glass. The magnifying glass pointer enables you to zoom in and out on the slide. Click the slide when the magnifier has a plus sign to zoom in. Click when the magnifier has a minus sign to return to the smaller size.

When you print from PowerPoint, you can change the printout orientation to match the layout of your slides.

PowerPoint assumes that you prefer your slides to have more room horizontally than vertically. This makes sense because most slides consist of just a few bullet points (so you do not need much room vertically), but some or all of those bullet points might be long (so you need more room horizontally).

A slide orientation that gives you more room horizontally than vertically is called *landscape*, and it is the default orientation in PowerPoint. If your slide content needs more room vertically than horizontally — for example, to fit in more bullets or tall pictures — then you need to switch to *portrait* orientation. You can set one orientation for slides and another for all other page formats: notes, handouts, and outlines.

CHANGE SLIDE ORIENTATION

1 Click the Design tab.

2 Click Slide Orientation.

3 Click the desired orientation.

The slides change to the new orientation for printing.

CHANGE ORIENTATION FOR OTHER PAGES

4 Click Office.

5 Point to the arrow button at the right of the Print choice.

6 Click Print Preview.

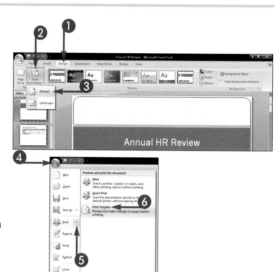

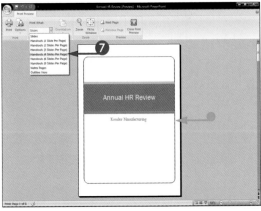

- The Print Preview appears, showing the new slide orientation.

⑦ Click the Print What drop-down list and select another type of print output to view, if needed.

⑧ Click the Orientation button to choose another print orientation for handouts, notes, or outline pages.

⑨ Click the Print button to open the Print dialog box so that you can continue printing.

Try This!
PowerPoint considers the paper size setting to be a function of your printer. So, to change paper size, open the Print dialog box by clicking Print in the Print Preview or by clicking Print on the Office menu. Make sure the correct printer is selected in the Name text box, and then click the Properties button. Properties differ for every printer, so look for a Paper Size choice, or click the Advanced button.

When your presentation is complete, you can print out a hard copy. PowerPoint gives you a number of printing options. For example, you can select the appropriate printer for your presentation. If you have a color printer available, you can print slides in color. You also have a choice in the slides that print. PowerPoint can print the current slide, all the selected slides, a range of slides, or your entire presentation. Finally, you can also choose the number of copies to print. Whatever options you choose, note that slides always print one per page, so the number of pages that will print will be the number of slides you choose to print multiplied by the number of copies. Remember, too, that slides will print with the orientation specified on the Design tab.

① Click Office.

② Click Print.

The Quick Print choice, which is on the Quick Access toolbar and the Print submenu, sends the presentation to the current printer without opening the Print dialog box.

The Print dialog box appears.

③ Make sure the desired printer is selected here.

④ To print selected slides, click the Slides option button and then specify which slides to print.

⑤ Change the Number of Copies to print, if needed.

Make sure Slides is selected from the Print What drop-down list.

⑥ Click OK.

The slides print to the specified printer.

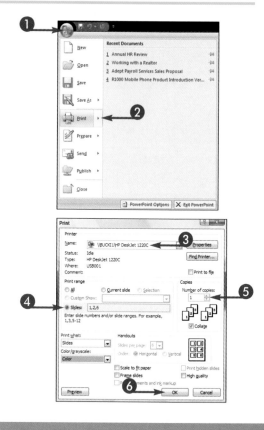

You can print slides with a frame, which places a neat borderline around the edge of the slides and defines them on a printed page.

By default, slides print without any kind of border around them. This is usually what you want because most slides consist of a white background and some text, and this content looks natural as it is on a printed page. However, if you use a

background color, pattern, texture, or image, the background appears to come to an abrupt halt at the edges of each slide, which can make slides look artificial. You can overcome this problem by *framing* the slides, which puts a thin border around the edges of each slide. This helps to contain the background, which makes your printouts more attractive.

1 Click Office.
2 Click Print.

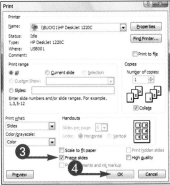

The Print dialog box opens.

3 Click the Frame slides check box to check it.

Make sure Slides is selected from the Print What drop-down list.

4 Click OK.

The slides print with frames.

You can print handouts as an aid for your audience. This may not be necessary for a short, simple presentation in which audience members are content to watch and then perhaps ask a few questions at the end. For longer, more complex presentations, however, you need to help out your audience by providing them with handouts, which show thumbnail versions of your slide, usually six per page.

Presentation handouts help audience members follow along and give them a place where they can take notes for future reference.

You can print from one to nine slides on a handout page. Note, too, that printing several slides per page can save paper when you want to print handouts for a lengthy presentation.

① Click Office.

② Click Print.

The Print dialog box appears.

③ Click here and select Handouts from the Print what drop-down list.

④ Click here and select the number of Slides per page to print.

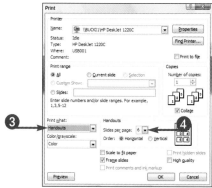

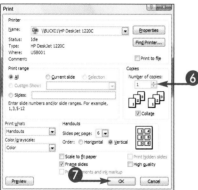

The preview changes to reflect the number of slides you selected.

⑤ Click an option button to specify if you want slides to print in Horizontal or Vertical order.

Vertical prints slides in order down the left column, continuing in order down the right column.

Note: *This option is available to you only if you select four or more slides per handout in step 4.*

⑥ Confirm the proper Number of copies and other settings.

⑦ Click OK.

The handouts print.

Customize It!

PowerPoint offers several ways to customize your handouts using the Handout Master. For example, in Master view you can reposition the placeholders for the various handouts. Also, you can use the Master to make changes to the overall handout appearance. Use the check boxes in the Placeholders group on the Handout Master tab as well as the Header & Footer button on the Insert tab to control header and footer appearance for printed handouts. See Chapter 4 for more about working with masters.

You can save costs and speed up the print operation by printing your presentation either in black and white or in grayscale.

It is a rare presentation these days that is not a colorful affair with interesting background effects, images, colored text, and so on. This is wonderful for electronic presenting, but it can cause problems if you need to print out the presentation because color printing is expensive and slow. As an alternative, PowerPoint enables you to print a presentation in either grayscale or black and white. Grayscale provides some shading to help you see graphic and background elements. Black and white shows no such shading and will show no background color or pattern. Note, too, that for draft printouts, using grayscale or black and white reduces the use of more expensive color inks.

① Click Office.

② Click Print.

The Print dialog box appears.

③ Click here and select either Grayscale or Pure Black and White.

④ Optionally, you may select other print settings as desired.

⑤ Click OK.

The presentation prints with your color selection.

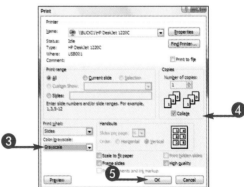

If your presentation includes hidden slides, you can force PowerPoint to print them.

You may decide not to show every slide in a presentation. For example, if a benefits presentation includes manager information but you are showing it to hourly workers, you can hide the manager slides. If you want to include printouts to

go along with this presentation, you have to make sure that you do not include the hidden slides in the print job. Unfortunately, PowerPoint's default setting is to print hidden slides. Therefore, you must turn off this setting if you do not want hidden slides printed.

① Click Office.

② Click Print.

The Print dialog box appears.

③ Click the Print hidden slides check box.

④ Click OK.

The presentation prints with or without hidden slides, as specified.

Note: *If there are no hidden slides in your presentation, this option is not available.*

You can print just the outline of your presentation. This is useful for those times when you just want to focus on the presentation text and not the graphic details. Printing the outline is a good option in such a case.

When PowerPoint prints the outline, it prints only what you see when you switch to the Outline tab. (See Chapter 1 for a complete look at using the Outline tab and building a presentation outline.) In other words, the printed outline includes the slide titles, subtitles, and bullet points, but does not include images, charts, SmartArt, or any text entered in text boxes or footers.

① Click Office.

② Click Print.

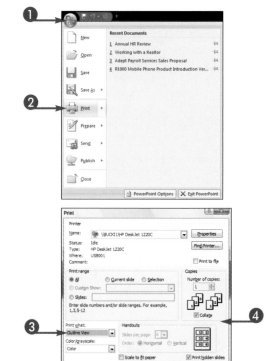

The Print dialog box appears.

③ Click here and select Outline View.

④ Optionally, you can change other print settings as desired.

⑤ Click OK.

The presentation outline prints.

Print Notes

Chapter 9: Print Presentations

You can give yourself a printout to reference during a rehearsal or presentation by printing out your notes pages.

The slide show presenter often needs a cheat sheet with important points to remember, additional facts, the answers to questions that the audience may pose. A good presenter will use the notes page (entered in the Notes pane of Normal view) of each slide to record such information. You can then print those notes pages with each slide at the top of a page and any notes for that slide below. The speaker can reference the notes pages during the presentation or a rehearsal.

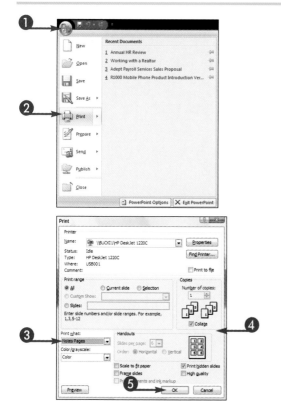

① Click Office.

② Click Print.

The Print dialog box appears.

③ Click here and select Notes Pages.

④ Optionally, you can choose other print settings as desired.

⑤ Click OK.

The slides and notes are printed.

Publish Presentations

With PowerPoint you can publish a presentation for the Web without using a Web publishing program. You can save the Web presentation to your hard disk and preview it there, or transfer it directly to a Web server.

When you use the commands to publish a presentation, you essentially save the presentation in a Web file format. Once you post the presentation and its supporting files to a Web server, people can access it at any time from around the world. Keep in mind that the Web presentation typically consists of an HTML (HyperText Markup Language) file and folders holding other necessary files such as clip art or other pictures used in the presentation.

For others to access the presentation online, the presentation files must be placed on a Web (http://) server computer. In some cases, you can publish the files directly from the Save As dialog box to a Web server. Contact your ISP (Internet Service Provider) or company Webmaster to learn the address to use for publishing the files.

When you save the presentation as a single Web page file or in the more traditional format of an HTML file with support files, the presentation automatically offers certain navigation features to those viewing it in a Web browser program.

Quick Tips

Save a Presentation as a Single Web Page File

For convenience — especially if you must upload your Web presentation manually — you can save your presentation in single Web file format.

If your presentation is not too large, you can make it easier to distribute the presentation and for others to open the presentation by combining all the slides, images, and other presentation objects into a single Web page file. To do this,

you use PowerPoint's Single File Web Page format. This is the MHTML — MIME HTML — format. It combines the HTML and references to external files such as images into a single file that uses the .mht extension. You can easily e-mail the MHTML file to someone who wishes to view the presentation. The recipient can then double-click the MHTML file to view it in a browser.

① Click Office.

② Click Save As.

The Save As dialog box appears.

③ Navigate to the folder in which you want to save the file.

④ Click here and select Single File Web Page.

⑤ Type in a file name.

⑥ Click Save.

PowerPoint saves the presentation as a single MHTML Web page file.

You can use Windows and the Web browser installed on your system to view the Web page that you saved.

Before you send a presentation as an MHTML file to another person, you should make sure that the file operates properly. That is, you need to try out different scenarios to ensure that the file can be opened and that it looks the way you want. Ideally, you should test the

MHTML file on all the Web browsers installed on your system. If you have other computers you can use, you should install a variety of systems and Web browsers so that you can test the MHTML file in different setups. In each case, make sure that the layout, color, fonts, and other presentation features display correctly.

① From the Windows desktop, open a folder window.

② Navigate to the folder that holds the presentation MHTML file.

③ Double-click the file or its icon, depending on the folder view.

If you see a prompt about whether to proceed, click the option or link for doing so. If a yellow Information Bar appears near the top of the browser window, click it and then click the Allow Blocked Content (or similar) choice and then respond to any additional prompts to continue.

Your Web browser displays the presentation.

④ After viewing and testing the presentation, click Close.

You can gain more control over the conversion of your presentation to the Web format if you publish the page to the Web.

Besides the MHTML, PowerPoint enables you to save your presentation using the Web Page format. This is a regular HTML Web page that uses the .htm file extension. PowerPoint also creates a folder named *Filename*_files — where *Filename* is the file name of the presentation — that includes any supporting files, such as images required by the presentation slides. You can set options for the Web site and publish directly to the Web server.

① Click Office.

② Click Save As.

The Save As dialog box appears.

③ Click here and edit the file name, if desired.

④ Click here and select Web Page.

⑤ Click Publish.

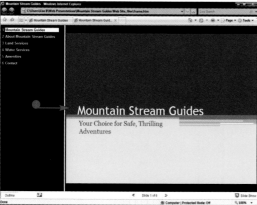

The Publish as Web Page dialog box appears.

6 Click options to control whether to include all slides and/or speaker notes.

7 Type the location in which you want to save the Web presentation files.

● You also can click the Browse button to specify a folder on the system.

8 To have the finished presentation open in your Web browser, click Open published Web page in browser.

9 Click Publish.

● Respond to any prompts about ActiveX controls as needed. Your presentation opens in the Web browser installed on your system.

Note: *See the section "Navigate a Presentation in a Browser" to learn to use the onscreen controls for working with the presentation.*

More Options!

By default, PowerPoint uses the presentation's file name as the title of the Web presentation. You can change that title to something more interesting or useful. In the Save As dialog box, before you click Publish, click Change Title, type the presentation title you want to use, and then click OK. Then proceed with publishing the presentation.

When you publish your presentation to the Web, you can configure the resulting Web page to be compatible with whatever browsers your audience uses.

Different Web browsers display information differently. For example, earlier versions of Internet Explorer cannot display some graphics formats accurately. Similarly, later versions of Internet Explorer implement some features that are not supported by earlier versions of Netscape Navigator. If you know which browser version viewers of your Web site are likely to be using, you should select which browsers to support to ensure that the presentation displays optimally for most people.

① In the Save As dialog box, click here and select Single File Web Page or Web Page as the Save as type.

② Click Publish.

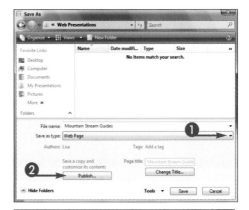

The Publish as Web Page dialog box appears.

③ Click the Web browser option you expect most of your Web site viewers to use.

④ Click Publish.

PowerPoint saves the presentation and displays it in your Web browser if that option is selected.

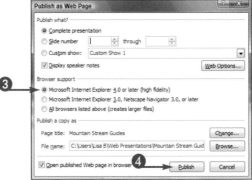

When viewing a presentation in a Web browser, you can take advantage of the controls displayed by the browser to navigate the presentation.

When you save a presentation for the Web, you can view the resulting HTML or MHTML file in a Web browser. The Web presentation offers tools for moving from slide to slide. In most cases, you get arrow buttons to move forward and backward through the slides; you get an

Outline pane that enables you to jump to a slide by clicking it; you can toggle the Outline pane on and off, and you can expand and collapse the outline to show more or less detail. You can also start and stop narration and display presentation in Full Screen mode.

Whether you saved a presentation to your disk or published it to a Web server, you should view your Web presentation for appearance and proper operation.

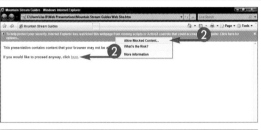

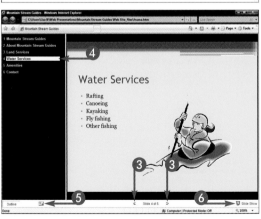

① To open your presentation file, double-click the HTML or MHTML file, or navigate to the address for the Web presentation.

② Respond to any display prompts that appear.

The presentation appears in the browser window.

③ Click the Next Slide arrow to move forward or the Previous Slide arrow to move backward one slide at a time.

④ Click a slide title in the Outline pane to navigate to that slide.

⑤ Click Expand/Collapse Outline to show more or less of the presentation outline.

⑥ Click Slide Show to display the presentation in Full Screen Slide Show format.

You can press Esc to exit Full Screen mode or close your Web browser to finish viewing the Web presentation.

You can ensure that other people see your Web-based presentation as you intended it by specifying fonts that the browser should use in case your presentation fonts are not available on the readers' systems.

PowerPoint displays presentations using fonts installed on your system. Sometimes those fonts are not available when others

view the presentation online. You can set which fonts to substitute in a Web presentation when needed. You can choose from proportional and fixed-width fonts.

Proportional fonts have letters that use varying widths. In a *fixed-width* font, every letter has the same width.

---

① In the Save As dialog box, click here and select Single File Web Page or Web Page as the Save as type.

② Click Publish.

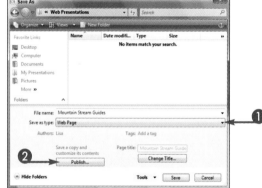

The Publish as Web Page dialog box appears.

③ Click Web Options.

The Web Options dialog box appears.

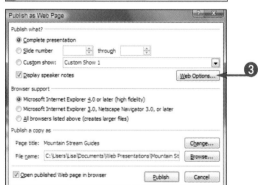

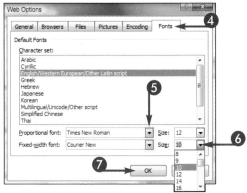

4 Click the Fonts tab.

5 Click here and select the desired fonts.

6 Click here and select the font size for the chosen font.

7 Click OK.

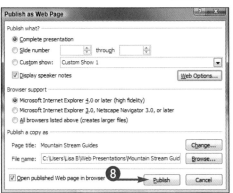

PowerPoint saves the font settings and redisplays the Publish as Web Page dialog box.

8 Click Publish.

PowerPoint publishes the pages with your substitute font choices.

Did You Know?

If a browser cannot recognize a font in your presentation, it uses the specified proportional or fixed-width font. By selecting a default font for each of these that most closely resembles the fonts used in your presentation, you ensure that your Web presentation looks as close as possible to your design. Try using Times New Roman, Arial, Symbol, or Courier. Most browsers have no problem reading these.

Customize Colors for Web Presentations

You can give your Web-based presentation a bit more visual interest by customizing the colors that the browser uses to display the text in the Outline and Notes panes.

By default, an online presentation uses a black background and white text in the Outline pane and the Notes pane. Unfortunately, this plain color scheme might clash with your presentation colors.

To avoid that, you can configure the Web presentation to use colors that match your presentation colors. Alternatively, you can switch to a white background with black text or you can use the colors a user has set for his or her browser. You also can use the presentation's accent color for text.

---

① In the Save As dialog box, click here and select Single File Web Page or Web Page as the Save as type.

② Click Publish.

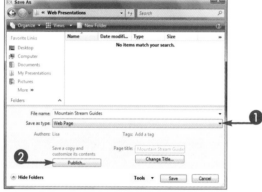

The Publish as Web Page dialog box appears.

③ Click Web Options.

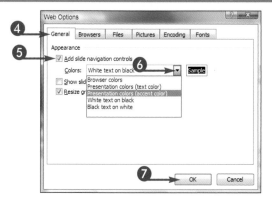

The Web Options dialog box appears.

④ Click the General tab, if needed.

⑤ Click the Add slide navigation controls check box, if unchecked.

⑥ Click here and select the color scheme to use.

⑦ Click OK to return to the Publish as Web Page dialog box.

⑧ Click Publish.

PowerPoint publishes the presentation with the selected colors.

More Options!

You can prevent the Outline pane from appearing in your Web presentation. In the Web Options dialog box used in the preceding steps, deselect the Add slide navigation controls check box. Alternatively, make sure people run the show in Slide Show mode. The latter is probably a better option because it provides the option of using the navigation tools.

You can convert one or more slides into a graphics format for use in other applications.

There may be instances where a recipient cannot view presentation information on the Web, or where you may want to include images of slides in another document such as a Word document. You can save one or all of the slides in a presentation as a graphic file. PowerPoint supports several graphics formats, including GIF, JPEG, TIFF, and PNG. You can import all of these file formats into other Office applications. If you want to use a slide image in a Web page, your best bet is either GIF or JPEG, which are the standard Web graphics formats.

① If you want to publish a single slide as a graphic, select that slide in Normal view.

② Click Office.

③ Click Save As.

The Save As dialog box appears.

④ Click here.

⑤ Click the desired graphics file format.

Note: *To specify other save options, see the section "Save a Presentation as a Single Web Page."*

⑥ Click Save.

PowerPoint asks whether you want to save all slides or a selected slide.

● If you selected a single slide to save in Step **1**, click Current Slide Only.

● Otherwise, click Every Slide.

PowerPoint saves the slides as graphic files.

A message box appears telling you that the slides have been saved.

7 Click OK.

Try It!

To use one of the slide graphic files, you can either insert a reference to the file in a Web page, or you can insert the file into a document in another application. In most applications, you can use an insert command or button to find and insert graphics files. For example, in Microsoft Office Word 2007, click the Insert tab on the Ribbon, and then click the Picture button to open the Insert Picture dialog box. Locate the slide picture file, click it, and then click Insert.

Finalizing and Making a Presentation

Before you present your PowerPoint slide show, you should be sure you understand the tools available to make things flow smoothly during your presentation. A successful live presentation requires solid content, good design, and a prepared presenter. Preparing to make a presentation involves double-checking your presentation for problems and getting yourself comfortable with your material and presentation environment.

Nothing is more embarrassing than displaying a slide in front of an audience only to find that your company's name is misspelled. Checking your slides for details such as spelling, grammatical usage, and

typos can save you a lot of embarrassment at show time. Print the presentation outline to review the text so that you are not distracted by design elements. Also, have somebody else who is not as close to the presentation review it. That person may catch errors you have missed.

Practicing your presentation several times before you give it in front of an audience makes you feel more comfortable with the material and your own presentation style. Rehearse in front of a mirror or a friend, or even record yourself with a video camera and play the recording back. You can spot irritating mannerisms or expressions and try to avoid them.

Quick Tips

When you create a presentation by entering text and graphics elements and animations on slides, you need only start Slide Show view to run the show. You can end the show at any time or view all of the slides.

Before starting, always check your timing and, if you must, edit your presentation or change the pacing to fit the time you have. Use the Rehearse Timings feature

(see Chapter 8) to walk through your presentation and record the time you take to cover each slide. Also, be sure to check those all-important slide show settings, covered in Chapter 8. You should set up ahead of time the format for the presentation; which slides to include, monitors and resolution; and how you will control the advancement from slide to slide.

START A SHOW

① Click the View Tab.

② Click Slide Show.

The slide show starts with the currently selected slide.

To start the slide show, you can also press F5.

To start from the beginning, select the first slide in the presentation before starting the show.

END A SHOW

① To end the show before you reach the last slide, click the Slide Show Menu button.

② Click End Show.

The slide show closes.

You can also press Esc to end the show at any time.

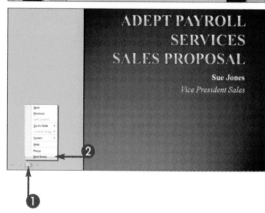

You can use a shortcut menu or onscreen tools to move through a slide show that you're presenting. You also can use your right and left arrow keys to move forward and backward. On the shortcut menu, PowerPoint offers four main navigation methods: Next, Previous, Last Viewed, and Go to Slide. Click Next to move to the next slide in the presentation; click

Previous to move to the previous slide in the presentation; click Last Viewed to jump to the last slide displayed in the presentation — this will be different from the previous slide if you used a hyperlink or action button to jump from a different slide; and click Go to Slide to display a menu of the slides in the presentation, and you then click the slide you want to view.

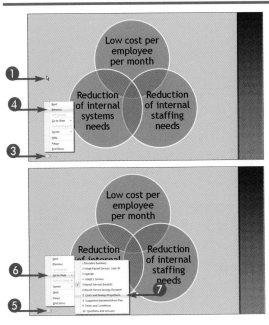

① With a presentation in Slide Show view, move the mouse.

The Presentation toolbar appears.

② Press the right arrow on the keyboard to display the next slide.

③ Click the Slide Show Menu button.

④ Click Previous.

PowerPoint displays the previous slide.

⑤ Click the Slide Show Menu button.

⑥ Click Go to Slide.

⑦ Click a slide title.

PowerPoint displays the slide you selected.

Using the Pointer

PowerPoint enables you to use a technology called ink to draw freehand on your screen during a presentation. You use a pointer tool to do this. You can use ink to highlight or annotate an important point or to jot down ideas that come up during your interaction with the audience. PowerPoint offers three different pen styles — Ballpoint Pen, Felt Tip Pen, and

Highlighter. You can also choose from a wide variety of pen colors.

If you make a mistake while annotating, PowerPoint also offers an Eraser tool that you can use to remove individual annotations. You can also use the Erase All Ink on Slide tool to clear the slide of annotations.

CHOOSE A POINTER STYLE

① With a slide show running, click the Pointer menu button on the Presentation toolbar.

Note: *See the section "Navigate Among Slides" to display the presentation toolbar.*

② Click a pointer style.

Ballpoint Pen produces a thinner drawing line.

Felt Tip Pen gives a little thicker drawing line.

Highlighter provides a transparent color wash.

Arrow displays your normal mouse pointer. You cannot draw any annotations with this option.

③ Drag onscreen with the mouse.

Either a line or a highlight appears, depending on your choice of pointer style.

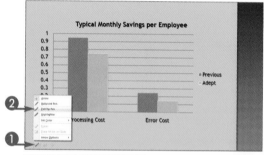

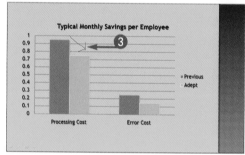

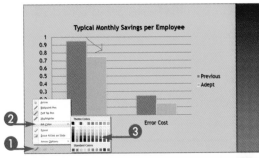

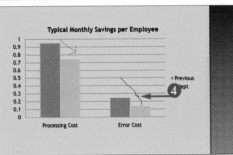

CHANGE INK COLOR

① Click the Pointer menu button on the Presentation toolbar.

② Point to Ink Color.

A color palette appears.

③ Click a color swatch.

④ Drag your mouse to write or draw an annotation.

The annotation appears in the new ink color.

Remove It!

To remove annotations from a slide, use the Erase features. Click the Pointer menu button, and then click Erase All Ink on Slide to clear all annotations on the currently displayed slide. Or you can click Eraser on the Pointer menu, which turns on the Eraser tool. Now drag the mouse pointer over only the annotations you want to erase. When you are done, click Eraser on the Pointer menu again to turn it off.

You can save slide show annotations so that they appear the next time you run the show. Most of the time, the annotations you make during a slide show are temporary. For example, you might draw a freehand arrow to point out something important in a chart. Similarly, you might add a bit of text to clarify something for the audience. For these annotations, you can erase them one by one, or you can choose not to save any of them. Choose either approach when prompted at the end of the slide show.

Sometimes, however, your annotations add useful content and context to your slides. In this case, you may want the annotations to appear again in future shows. Rather than re-creating them, you can have PowerPoint save the annotations along with your presentation.

1 With a slide show running and annotations drawn on some slides, click the Slide Show Menu button.

Note: *See the section "Navigate Among Slides" to display the Presentation toolbar.*

2 Click End Show.

Or, in place of steps 1 and 2, simply finish showing the entire slide show.

The Microsoft Office PowerPoint dialog box appears.

3 Click to discard or keep the annotations.

The dialog box and slide show close.

You cannot erase annotations when you next run the show. To delete a saved annotation, select the annotation in the Slide pane in Normal view and delete it.

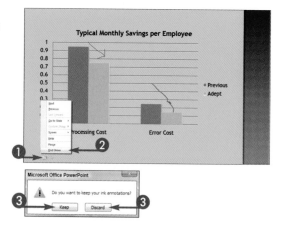

If you need help running your show after starting it, you need not stop the show and open PowerPoint Help. Slide Show view offers a single help screen with the shortcuts for running the show and managing presentation features such as pointer options. There are many of these shortcuts, so it is difficult to memorize them all. For example, you can press N to advance to the next slide or animation; you can press P to return to the previous slide or animation; you can press a number and then Enter to navigate to that slide number; and you can press A to toggle the mouse pointer and slide show navigation tools on and off. If you cannot remember these shortcuts, display the Slide Show Help window to get a quick reminder.

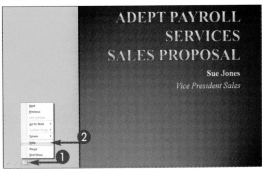

① With a slide show running, click the Slide Show Menu button.

② Click Help.

The Help window appears.

③ Look up the shortcut on the left to perform the procedure you want, which is listed on the right.

④ Click OK.

The Help window closes.

Work with Multiple Monitors and Presenter View

You can configure PowerPoint to use two monitors for your presentation — one that only you see and one the audience sees. In the monitor that you see, you can perform some other action. The most common scenario is to use your monitor to display Presenter view and use its tools to make running a show easier. Presenter view shows a screen split into three sections: one for the current slide, another for the current slide's Notes page, and a third that shows thumbnail images of the presentation's slides — you can use these thumbnails to look ahead in the presentation and to quickly navigate to a specific slide. The Presenter view also shows the slide show navigation tools.

SET UP MULTIPLE MONITORS

1. Click the Slide Show tab.
2. Click Set Up Slide Show.

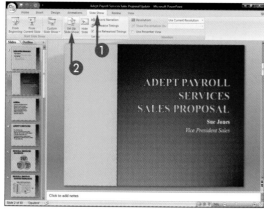

The Set Up Show dialog box displays.

3. Click here and select the monitor to show the presentation on.

4. Click the Show Presenter View check box.

5. Click OK.

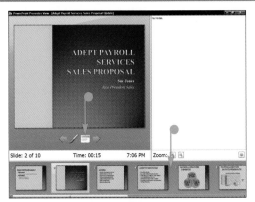

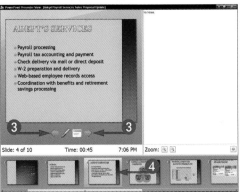

USE PRESENTER VIEW

1 Click the View tab.

2 Click Slide Show.

The slide show begins playing.

● The presenter's monitor shows the Presenter view, with tools for navigating in and delivering the presentation.

3 Click an arrow button to move forward and backward through the slides.

Note: The two slide show control buttons that appear under the current slide enables you to work with annotation settings and navigate the show.

4 Click a slide thumbnail to jump to that slide.

5 Press Esc at any time to end the presentation.

The specified resolution is set when you run your slide show.

More Options!

If your computer has a video adapter with a graphics coprocessor, it can help speed up the display on your monitor. If you have such hardware in your computer, click the Slide Show tab, then click Set Up Slide Show to display the Set Up Show dialog box. Click to activate the Use Hardware Graphics Acceleration option, and then click OK. Look in your owner's manual or check the list of hardware drivers in Windows Control Panel to see whether an accelerator is available to you.

Making a Photo Album

Sometimes a presentation should rely more heavily on pictures than on text, tables, or graphs. For example, if you have a series of photos illustrating a process, you might want to create a training presentation using those photos. In such a case, you can save time and take advantage of some special layout features by setting up the presentation as a photo album.

As with a regular presentation, the details matter when you want to use and share a photo album presentation. After you use the tasks in this chapter to create your photo album, follow through with some last steps to ensure that your photo presentation has the level of professionalism you seek. For

example, by default, PowerPoint uses a blank presentation as the foundation for a photo album slide show. This means that the title slide and any other inserted slides have a plain white background. At a minimum, consider adding a theme or background to the slides without photos. Chapter 3 explains how to do so.

In addition, if you imported your album photos from a digital camera or got them from another person, do not assume that all the pictures use the correct orientation. Review each slide and picture in the slide show. If a picture uses the wrong orientation, correct it as described in the section, "Work with Photos."

Quick Tips

If you have a collection of related pictures on your computer, you can turn those pictures into a photo album. Most PowerPoint presentations consist of some combination of text, tables, charts, and perhaps an image or two. However, you may occasionally need to create a presentation that consists solely of pictures. For example, rather than writing down the a various steps in a process, you could use a series of pictures to illustrate that process.

Similarly, if you are introducing a new line of products, you might want a presentation that just shows images of those products

You can create these and similar presentations by creating a photo album, which is a presentation geared toward presenting pictures or illustrations. You can use the Photo Album command to create and format the picture slides for a photo album.

① Click the Insert tab.

② Click the Photo Album button.

Clicking the bottom portion of the button that displays a menu.

The Photo Album dialog box appears.

③ Click File/Disk.

The Insert New Pictures dialog box appears.

④ Navigate to the folder that holds the image files you want to insert into the album.

⑤ Select the picture files to insert.

Note: You can Shift+click or Ctrl+click to select multiple image files in the list.

⑥ Click Insert.

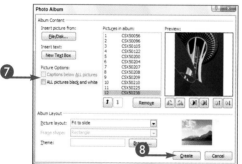

The Photo Album dialog box now lists the specified photos.

⑦ Adjust the photo album by choosing the desired settings.

⑧ Click Create.

PowerPoint creates the photo album presentation.

Did You Know?

You can apply a theme or other formatting to the photo album, insert additional slides as needed, run the photo album presentation as an onscreen slide show, and more. The key difference is that you can use the Photo Album or Edit Photo album dialog boxes to set up a picture layout or frame all the slides. You also can use the dialog box to reorder the pictures or make changes to picture settings such as rotation.

Create an Album with Pictures from a Digital Camera

If you have a collection of related pictures on your digital camera, you can import those pictures into PowerPoint and use them as part of a photo album. For example, if you attend a trade show or conference and take a number of pictures with your digital camera, you might want to present those pictures as a photo album.

Creating a photo album with images from your digital camera saves you the step of transferring images from the camera to your computer's hard disk when building your photo album. PowerPoint will, in effect, directly import the pictures into the album, where you can rearrange and work with them as needed.

---

① Attach the digital camera to the computer via its cable, and turn the camera to its playback or transfer setting.

Note: *If Windows Vista displays an Importing Pictures and Videos dialog box, click Close to close it, and then click Yes.*

② In PowerPoint, click the Insert tab.

③ Click the Photo Album button.

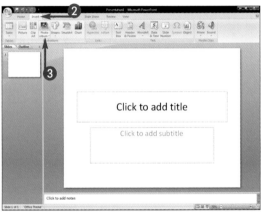

The Photo Album dialog box appears.

④ Click File/Disk.

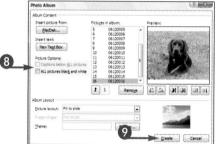

The Insert New Pictures dialog box appears.

⑤ Navigate to the folder containing the image files you want to insert into the album.

Note: Most digital cameras are listed as a Removable Disk. Many digital cameras organize pictures in dated folders within the DCIM folder.

⑥ Select the picture files to insert.

⑦ Click Insert.

PowerPoint imports the photos. The Photo Album dialog box now lists the specified photos.

⑧ Adjust the photo album by choosing the desired settings.

⑨ Click Create.

PowerPoint creates the photo album presentation.

⑩ Power down and disconnect your digital camera.

Did You Know?
The time PowerPoint takes to transfer the photos is a function of the photo size as well as the interface used — USB is faster than serial, for example. Today's multimegapixel digital cameras can take very high-quality images, but those image files are very large and transfer more slowly to a computer. If this is an ongoing issue for you, you can either shoot your pictures using lower size and quality settings on your camera, or transfer the images and use an image-editing program to reduce image size before making the photo album.

You can customize your photo album by choosing the number of pictures you want to appear on each slide, including titles with each slide, and add a frame around the pictures. Setting up each slide to display one, two, or four pictures per slide is one of the best aspects of a photo album, because it saves you the time and trouble of having to plug photos individually into a custom slide layout.

If each slide has a different theme, then it is a good idea to include titles on each slide and use those titles to name or describe the themes. Finally, selecting a frame shape to apply to each slide is a great way to improve the appearance of the photos.

① With the photo album file open, click the Insert tab.

② Click the Photo Album down arrow.

③ Click Edit Photo Album.

You can also make these choices when you originally create the photo album.

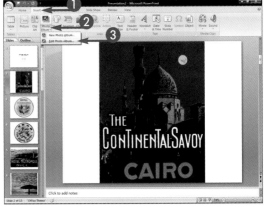

The Edit Photo Album dialog box appears.

④ Click here and select the picture layout.

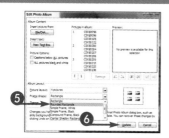

The Frame Shape choice becomes active.

⑤ Click here and select the frame.

⑥ Click Update.

● PowerPoint applies the new layout to the photo album slides, like the example shown here.

Did You Know?

When you create a photo album, PowerPoint automatically inserts the text By *Name* on the Title slide, where *Name* is most likely your name. PowerPoint gets this name from the User Name entered the first time PowerPoint was run. You can edit that on a one-time basis just by changing that text in the text placeholder on the slide. To change the user information overall, you will need to work with PowerPoint options, which are described in Chapter 13.

If you think you need more than just the pictures to communicate the message in your photo album presentation, you can add a text caption below each picture. The nature of a photo album presentation is that you will be describing each picture that you display. This means that in many cases you do not need extra text on each slide. However, if you opt to display multiple photos on each slide, you can make it easier to refer to each picture by providing captions.

You can also use captions to add descriptive or humorous labels to each picture, or to communicate information about the step or operation depicted in the photo. Finally, if your photo album will be part of a kiosk or other automatic display, captions can help viewers understand each picture.

① With the photo album file open, click the Insert tab.

② Click the Photo Album down arrow.

③ Click Edit Photo Album.

You can also make these choices when you originally create the photo album.

The Edit Photo Album dialog box appears.

④ Click here and select 1 Picture, 2 Pictures, or 4 Pictures.

Note: *The default layout, Fit to Slide, does not support captions.*

⑤ Click Captions below ALL pictures.

⑥ Click Update.

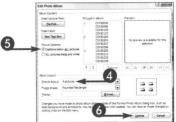

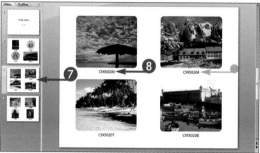

● The dialog box closes, and a placeholder caption appears below each photo.

⑦ Click the slide for which you want to edit captions.

⑧ Click the caption placeholder text.

⑨ Edit the caption as desired, just as you would text in any other placeholder.

⑩ Click outside the caption to finalize it.

⑪ Repeat steps **7** to **10** to edit remaining caption placeholders as desired.

Try This!

What do you do if you want some, but not all, of your photos to have captions? To accomplish this, first apply captions to all pictures as described in this task. After you have done that, navigate to a slide that contains a photo that does not require a caption, and then delete the placeholder text for that caption. Repeat this procedure for each photo that does not require a caption.

To ensure that your photo album has the correct sequence and look, you can rearrange the photos, rotate the images, and modify the contrast and brightness of each image. The ability to change the photo sequence and rotation is important if you have issues with the order and orientation of the photos in your photo album. This is often the case when you import the pictures directly from your digital camera, where the sequence and orientation are determined by how the photos were shot.

You can also use the Edit Photo Album dialog box to change the contrast and brightness of each photo. This is useful either to improve the quality of certain images, or to get a consistent look throughout the photo album. Note, too, that you can also use the Edit Photo Album dialog box to remove images from the album.

① With the photo album file open, click the Insert tab.

② Click the Photo Album down arrow.

③ Click Edit Photo Album.

The Edit Photo Album dialog box appears.

④ Click the photo you want to adjust.

⑤ To move the selected picture in the photo album, click the Up or Down button as needed.

Because PowerPoint does not list the pictures by caption, you may have to click various pictures in the list to preview and ensure you have arranged them in the proper order.

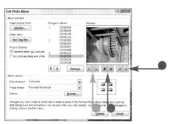

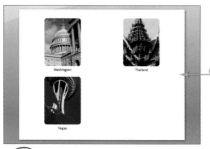

● To rotate the selected picture, click Rotate Counterclockwise or Rotate Clockwise.

● To change contrast for the selected picture, click Increase Contrast or Decrease Contrast.

● To change the brightness for the selected picture, click Increase Brightness or Decrease Brightness.

Note: Changes to rotation, contrast, and brightness do not affect your original photo files.

⑥ To take the selected picture out of the album, click Remove.

⑦ Click Update.

● PowerPoint closes the Edit Photo Album dialog box, applying your changes.

Reverse It!

If you accidentally delete a picture from the album, you can get it back, but how you do so depends on where you are in the update process. PowerPoint does not ask you to confirm a deletion after step 10. If you have not yet clicked Update in the Edit Photo Album dialog box, click Cancel. You will lose any other changes, but the photo will still be in the photo album. If you have accepted the changes, redisplay the Edit Photo Album dialog box, and then click the File/Disk button to find and add the photo back in.

You can add a text box to a photo album slide, and the text box fills one picture space within the picture layout on a slide. This is useful if you have more extensive information about the photo or photos on a particular slide. If that information cannot be included in the slide title or in the photo captions, then you need to add a text box and insert the text into it.

Adding a text box to a slide is also useful if you want to insert a blank space to push a picture from one slide to the next. For example, if you are using a 2-picture layout, you might find that a slide includes two unrelated images. In that case, insert a text box before the second image, and PowerPoint will move that photo to the next slide.

1 With the photo album file open, click the Insert tab.

2 Click the down arrow on the bottom section of the Photo Album button.

3 Click Edit Photo Album.

The Edit Photo Album dialog box appears.

4 Click the photo after which you want to insert the text box.

5 Click New Text Box.

6 Click Update.

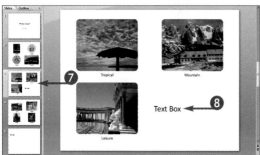

⑦ Click the slide that holds the text box to edit in Normal view.

⑧ Click the text box.

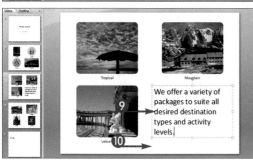

⑨ Edit the text box text as needed.

⑩ Click outside the text box to finish it.

Change It!

If you add a text box in the wrong place, you can fix the problem by moving the text box. Redisplay the Edit Photo Album dialog box and then click the text box in the Pictures in album list. Click the Up or Down buttons as many times a needed to move the text box to the desired location. Then click Update.

Customizing PowerPoint

PowerPoint is a powerful tool, and it becomes even more powerful when you know how to customize it to work the way you need it to. You can adjust various settings that streamline the way you use PowerPoint. For example, you can toggle the Mini toolbar and the Live Preview settings on and off, configure PowerPoint's ScreenTips, modify the PowerPoint color scheme, and change your user name. To ensure accurate spelling, you can also customize the spell checker as well as PowerPoint's AutoCorrect settings.

Another useful customization option you learn about in this chapter is setting the default view that PowerPoint uses when you open documents. For example, if you never use notes, you can tell PowerPoint not to show the Notes box. PowerPoint also offers a number of options that control slide shows, editing, printing, and AutoFormat, and you learn about those options in this chapter.

Finally, one of the secrets of PowerPoint productivity is an intimate knowledge of the Ribbon and its tabs. However, you can also customize aspects of the Ribbon to make it easier to use, and you learn about these customization techniques in this chapter.

Quick Tips

Modify Common PowerPoint Options

PowerPoint maintains a collection of what it calls "top options" for working with the program. You can improve a number of key aspects of PowerPoint by customizing these top options to suit the way you prefer to work.

Some of these options are common to working with a variety of features. For example, the Mini toolbar appears when you select any text in PowerPoint, the ScreenTips appear when you hover the mouse pointer over any Ribbon object, and the Live Preview feature shows you a preview of how an option affects the slide. You can toggle each of these features on and off. PowerPoint's top options also include the program color scheme, your user name, and the languages you want to use with PowerPoint. You can change these common options in the PowerPoint Options dialog box.

---

① Click the Office button.

② Click PowerPoint Options.

The PowerPoint Options dialog box appears.

③ Click Popular.

④ Slect your options for working with PowerPoint.

● Click here to turn the pop-up Mini toolbar on or off.

● Click here to select a style of ScreenTip to display.

● Click here to enable or disable Live Preview.

● Click here to select the program color scheme.

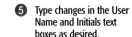

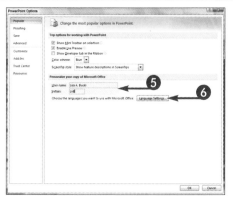

⑤ Type changes in the User Name and Initials text boxes as desired.

When you create a file, PowerPoint uses the User Name entry to identify you as the file's author.

⑥ Click Language Settings.

⑦ Click an editing language.

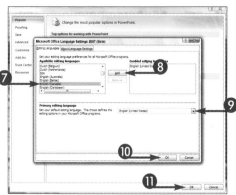

⑧ Click Add.

PowerPoint adds the language to the list of enabled editing languages.

⑨ Click here and select a primary editing language.

⑩ Click OK.

The Microsoft Office Language Settings dialog box closes.

⑪ Click OK.

The PowerPoint Options dialog box closes and applies your new settings.

TIP

More Options!

If you activate the Show Developer Tab check box, PowerPoint adds a Developer tab to the Ribbon. That tab offers choices for writing PowerPoint macros. If you later learn macro programming skills, you can use the tools on the Developer tab to not only create macros, but also to apply those macros to controls such as buttons and list boxes that you add to slides.

You can enhance spelling accuracy as well as make sure the spell checker does not interfere with your work by customizing the Office and PowerPoint spelling options.

The Office spelling options apply to all the Office programs, and you can use them to toggle whether Office spell checks uppercase words, words with numbers, Internet addresses, repeated words, and more. By default, PowerPoint's spelling checker constantly checks your spelling as you type. A red, wavy underline appears to identify a possible misspelling. You can turn off automatic spell checking and control the types of corrections enforced in the PowerPoint Options dialog box. Some users prefer to worry about spelling after developing all the text in a presentation.

① Click the Office button.

② Click PowerPoint Options.

The PowerPoint Options dialog box appears.

③ Click Proofing.

④ Click here to select options that determine whether the spelling checker will flag certain types of errors, such as repeated words or words that contain numbers.

PowerPoint automatically creates a custom dictionary when you add words during a spelling check. If you want to view or change the contents of your custom dictionary, click Custom Dictionaries, and then click Edit Word List.

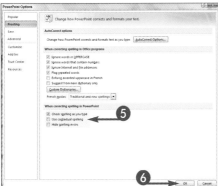

⑤ Click to specify PowerPoint's spell-checking preferences.

⑥ Click OK.

The dialog box closes and PowerPoint applies the new spelling changes.

More Options!

If you use many proper names and unique product names in your presentations, the spelling checker probably flags them as misspellings. To avoid this, open the PowerPoint Options dialog box, click the Proofing choice in the list at the left, and then click the Custom Dictionaries button. With the custom dictionary selected, click Edit Word List. Type each name to add in the CUSTOM.DIC dialog box that appears, and then click Add. Click OK three times to finish updating the dictionary.

Change AutoCorrect Settings

You can customize the AutoCorrect feature to have PowerPoint correct common typing or spelling errors rather than simply identifying them with a red wavy underline. AutoCorrect comes with a long list of predefined correction, such as spelling "the" as "teh," typing "can;t" instead of "can't," spelling "occasion" as "ocasion," and typing "cliche" instead of "cliché." However, you also can add corrections for your own poor habits, such as typing "actoin" when you meant to type "action."

You can also customize AutoCorrect by turning off some settings such as automatically capitalizing the first letter of sentences, or by deleting some of the predefined corrections, such as changing (c) to ©.

---

① Click the Office button.

② Click PowerPoint Options.

The PowerPoint Options dialog box appears.

③ Click Proofing.

④ Click AutoCorrect Options.

The AutoCorrect dialog box appears.

● If the AutoCorrect tab does not display, click it.

5 Click a check box to turn off any of the standard AutoCorrect features listed at the top of the dialog box.

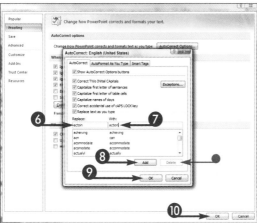

6 Type the misspelling.

7 Type the correct spelling.

8 Click Add.

● To delete a correction, click under Replace text as you type, and then click Delete.

9 Click OK.

The AutoCorrect dialog box closes.

10 Click OK.

The PowerPoint Options dialog box closes, and your AutoCorrect changes are saved.

Did You Know?

You may have some terms that you occasionally do not want AutoCorrect to fix. For example, you might use a term such as "acn" as an acronym in your company. However, AutoCorrect changes it to "can." Rather than deleting that AutoCorrect setting, use the Undo feature when you do not want to accept a correction. A keyboard shortcut that comes in handy is Ctrl+Z. After typing acn, when AutoCorrect changes it, press Ctrl+Z to change it back.

Customize Save Options

You can safeguard your work and make presentation files easier to share with other people by customizing PowerPoint's save option. For example, PowerPoint saves presentations in the PowerPoint 2007 file format. If you often share your presentations with a colleague who uses an older PowerPoint version, you can set the PowerPoint Presentation 97-2003 file format as the default. Similarly, you can also change the default location where PowerPoint saves your files to, say, a folder shared on your network.

To help ensure that you do not lose work, PowerPoint automatically saves AutoRecover information every 10 minutes. You can reduce that time to make your work even safer. You also can embed fonts in the saved presentation.

---

① Click the Office button.

② Click PowerPoint Options.

The PowerPoint Options dialog box appears.

③ Click Save.

④ Click here and select a file format.

When you save a new file, PowerPoint will by default use the specified format unless you choose another format in the Save As dialog box.

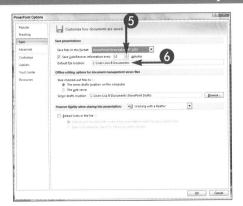

5 Click here to change the number of minutes between saving AutoRecover information.

Note: *Clicking to uncheck the Save AutoRecover Information check box turns off auto saving.*

6 If you want to save presentation files to a folder that is different than PowerPoint's default, click here and edit the Default file location text box entry.

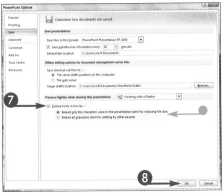

7 Click Embed fonts in the file.

PowerPoint saves fonts in the presentation file so that the presentation appears the same when viewed on a system lacking the fonts used in the presentation.

● You can specify whether to embed all characters or only those in use.

8 Click OK.

The dialog box closes and applies the new Save settings.

Did You Know?

Fonts install with the Windows operating system and programs like Microsoft Office. Four base fonts—Times New Roman, Arial, Symbol, and Courier New—are available to all Windows users automatically. Others, such as Book Antiqua or Garamond, are not available to every computer. If you use a particular font in a presentation and do not embed it, viewing the presentation on a computer without that font causes PowerPoint to replace it with a base font, which may throw off the presentation design.

Modify View and Slide Show Options

You can use PowerPoint's view options to customize the display of elements in the PowerPoint window. By default, PowerPoint displays the Slides/Outline tabs, the slide, and a notes box. You can select a custom view that displays the Outline tab by default, hides the notes box, shows only the slide, defaults to Slide Sorter view, and more. PowerPoint also enables you to specify the number of documents that appear on the Office menu's Recent Document list.

You can also use PowerPoint's slide show options to customize the defaults for running slide shows. For example, you can control whether the toolbar appears during slide show playback, whether a menu appears when you right-click, whether PowerPoint prompts you to keep ink annotations, and whether PowerPoint ends slide shows with a black slide.

---

① Click the Office button.

② Click PowerPoint Options.

The PowerPoint Options dialog box appears.

③ Click Advanced.

④ Click to select options affecting how PowerPoint displays presentations.

● You can click the spin box buttons to change the number of files displayed in the Recent Documents list at the right side of the File (the Office button) menu.

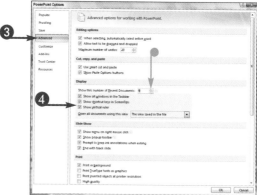

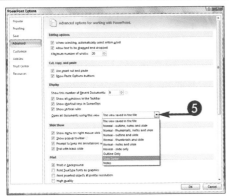

5 Click here and select a default view.

PowerPoint uses the specified view.

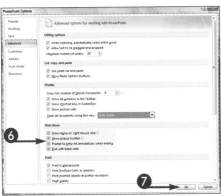

6 Click to select options affecting Slide Show preferences.

For example, the Show popup toolbar choice controls whether the navigation toolbar appears onscreen when you run the slide show.

7 Click OK.

The dialog box closes and applies the new settings.

Caution!
If you deactivate the Prompt to keep ink annotations when exiting check box, PowerPoint does not give you any way to save your annotations. The only way to save annotations is via the dialog box that appears at the end of the slide show to prompt you to save them. With that check box deselected in the PowerPoint Options dialog box, you can no longer save annotations.

You can customize PowerPoint's editing options to suit the way you work. For example, when you quickly drag your mouse across text to select it, PowerPoint automatically selects each work as you reach it. You can turn off this feature if you more often select only partial words. You can also turn off PowerPoint's feature that enables you to drag and drop text.

If you often use the Undo feature, you can customize the number of undos. The default is 20, but you can go as high as 150. PowerPoint also enables you to turn off the smart cut and paste feature, which automatically adds spaces when you paste text. Finally, you also can control the use of more recent features such as the Paste Options button, which appears when you paste a cut or copied object. Click it to see commands for working with the pasted selection.

① Click the Office button.

② Click PowerPoint Options.

The PowerPoint Options dialog box appears.

③ Click Advanced.

④ Click here to select the automatic selection of an entire word and whether to drag-and-drop.

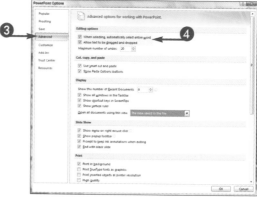

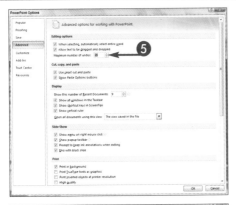

5 Click the Maximum number of undos spin box buttons to change number of times you can undo edits.

This feature consumes a lot of system memory, so if you feel PowerPoint's performance is slow, consider lowering this number.

6 Click to set options controlling the appearance of the Paste Options button, and smart cut and paste, a feature where PowerPoint adds missing spacing around pasted text or objects.

7 Click OK.

The dialog box closes, and PowerPoint applies the changes.

Did You Know?
The Paste Options button appears below a pasted object. It offers formatting options such as retaining the original source formatting or using design template formatting in the destination file or slide. Smart cut and paste helps to eliminate errors that can happen when you paste text or an object. Sometimes, if no spacing was selected around the cut or copied selection, it bumps up against other text when pasted. Smart cut and paste inserts missing space when pasted to eliminate that problem.

You can customize the way PowerPoint prints your presentations by modifying the print options. For example, you can configure PowerPoint to print TrueType fonts as graphics, which can speed up printing if your printer supports this feature. Also, you can print inserted graphics at the printer's resolution, which can improve the look of slide images.

You also can specify that a particular presentation always be printed with a particular printer and settings. These settings include what you want printed; whether you use color, grayscale, or black and white; and whether you print hidden slides, scale slides to fit the paper, and frame the slides. (See Chapter 9 for the details on these settings.) This saves you the trouble of choosing those settings every time you print that particular file.

① Click the Office button.

② Click PowerPoint Options.

The PowerPoint Options dialog box appears.

③ Click Advanced.

④ Scroll down to the bottom of the dialog box.

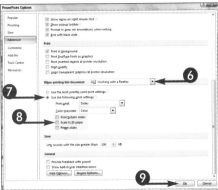

5 Click to select your print options.

● Print in background enables you to continue working in PowerPoint while printing.

● Print TrueType fonts as graphics changes how the printer handles fonts, which can speed up printing.

● Print inserted objects at printer resolution overrides the inserted object resolution settings in favor of the printer's.

6 Click here and select an open presentation file for which you want to set particular print settings.

7 Click Use the following print settings option to select it.

The rest of the choices become available.

8 Choose the desired setting for printing the selected presentation.

9 Click OK.

The dialog box closes, saving new settings.

TIP

Try This!

If you find that your presentations print slowly, you can try a couple of things. Enabling the Print in background option can slow down your printer, so you can try turning that feature off by clicking it to clear its check box. Also, if you have inserted graphic files with a low resolution but have Print inserted objects at printer resolution checked, that would actually be slowing down the printer because it would need to increase the graphics' resolutions.

Change AutoFormat Settings

You can customize PowerPoint's AutoFormat As You Type settings to set up this feature to suit the way you work. The AutoFormat feature works much like AutoCorrect, except that it corrects text formatting rather than text spelling. For example, AutoFormat automatically changes regular quotes with smart quotes; fractions written as separate characters (such as 1/2) with fraction symbols (such as ½); ordinals (such as 1st) with superscripts (such as 1st); two hyphens (--) with an emdash (—); and smiley faces with smiley symbols.

AutoFormat also applies formatting changes. For example, Internet addresses are converted to hyperlinks; lists of items are converted to bulleted or numbered lists; and title and body text are automatically fitted to their placeholders. You can turn these formatting changes off and back on as needed.

---

① Click the Office button.

② Click PowerPoint Options.

The PowerPoint Options dialog box appears.

③ Click Proofing.

④ Click AutoCorrect Options.

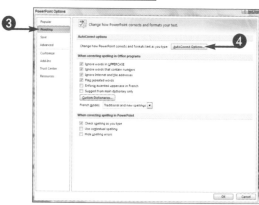

The AutoCorrect dialog box appears.

⑤ Click the AutoFormat As You Type tab.

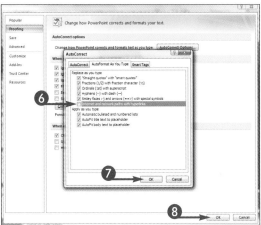

⑥ Click to select or deselect formatting choice.

⑦ Click OK.

The AutoCorrect dialog box closes.

⑧ Click OK.

The PowerPoint Options dialog box closes, applying the new settings.

More Options!

The AutoCorrect dialog box also includes a Smart Tags tab. Smart tags identify certain types of text with an underline. This tells you that if you click the text, such as a date, you can perform certain smart tag actions on it. The Smart Tags tab in the AutoCorrect dialog box enables you to turn smart tags on and download more smart tags if you like using them.

Customize the Quick Access Toolbar

You can get the most of the Quick Access toolbar by populating it with the commands that you use most often. The Quick Access toolbar appears to the right of the Office button in the upper-left corner of PowerPoint. By default, this toolbar offers buttons for the four most frequently used commands: Save, Undo, Repeat, and Quick Print. For even easier access than the Ribbon, you can customize the Quick Access toolbar by adding or removing buttons.

Note that you are not restricted to just a few commands. If you place the Quick Access toolbar below the Ribbon, then you can use the full width of the window, plus you get a More Controls button at the end of the toolbar that enables you to display a whole other row of commands.

① Click the Customize Quick Access Toolbar button.

② Click More Commands.

The PowerPoint Options dialog box appears, with the Customization choice displayed.

③ Click here and select the menu or category that holds the command button to add to the toolbar.

④ Click the command to add.

⑤ Click Add.

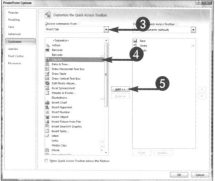

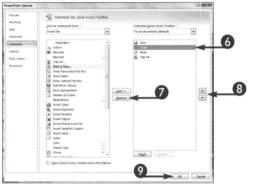

The command appears on the list of commands currently available on the Quick Access toolbar at the right.

⑥ Click a command to delete, move up, or move down in the list of commands currently on the toolbar.

⑦ Click Remove to remove it from the toolbar.

⑧ Click the Move Up or Move Down button to change a command's position.

⑨ Click OK.

● The PowerPoint Options dialog box closes, and the Quick Access toolbar shows its new command arrangement.

TIP

Reverse It!
You can revert the Quick Access toolbar to its default state if you do not like your customizations. Click the Customize Quick Access Toolbar button, and then click Customize Quick Access toolbar. Click the Reset button below the right list. Click Yes in the reset Customizations dialog box that appears, and then click OK to close the PowerPoint Options dialog box and view the Quick Access toolbar in its original form.

Hide and Redisplay Ribbon Commands

You can give yourself more room to display your slides by hiding the Ribbon when you are not using it. Whatever your opinion of the new Office 2007 Ribbon, there is no doubt that it seems to take up quite a bit of room at the top of each application window. There may be times when you require the maximum amount of vertical space possible to work with

your presentations. If you are not using the Ribbon, PowerPoint enables you to hide all of the Ribbon except for the tabs. This enables you to see more of the slide that you are working with.

When you need the Ribbon again, you can quickly redisplay it and continue with your work.

① Double-click the active tab on the Ribbon.

You also can press Ctrl+F1 to hide the Ribbon.

● The Ribbon commands disappear from the top of the screen, but the tabs remain visible.

② Double-click a Ribbon tab.

The Ribbon commands reappear. You can then click the button for the command you want.

● You can drag the Zoom slider or click one of the zoom controls to its right to change the zoom for the current slide.

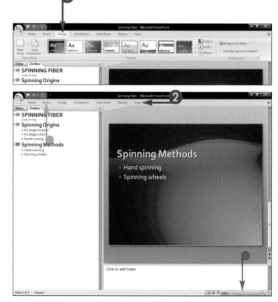

You can navigate PowerPoint quickly with a keyboard by taking advantage of the Ribbon's built-in KeyTips. If you find that operating PowerPoint via the keyboard as much as possible is faster and more efficient, then you know that one of the most frustrating things about previous versions of PowerPoint was the inability to select most toolbar buttons using the keyboard. Instead, you had to hunt through the menu system for the

equivalent command, or press the command's keyboard shortcut, if one existed for that feature.

One of the most useful new innovations in PowerPoint 2007 is the fact that every tab, group, and control on the Ribbon is accessible via the keyboard. The feature that makes this possible is called KeyTips, which are small tooltip-like banners that display over each object and that tell you which key (or keys) to press to select that object.

① Press Alt.

● The KeyTips (shortcut keys) for the Ribbon tabs and Quick Access toolbar appear in boxes beside the tabs and toolbar choices.

② Press the shortcut key for the tab you want to select on the keyboard.

In this example, G was pressed to display the Design tab.

● The tab appears with its available shortcut keys identified in boxes.

Note: To hide the tab shortcut keys, press Esc. To hide all shortcut keys, press Esc twice.

③ Press the shortcut key for the command you want to select.

In this example, pressing TC selects the Colors button. The command executes or a dialog box appears so that you can finish choosing command options.

Index

continued

Index

Index

Index